CROCODILES AT THE WATER COOLER

I give infinite thanks to God,
who has been pleased to make me the first
observer of marvelous things.
Galileo Galilei

A book is made possible through the support of our business colleagues who we work with, our friends who energize us and family who are the closest to us.

We would like to take a minute to thank all those who supported us including:

Patrick, Brenda & Ashley Jodon, Allan Custodio & Courtney Peal, Oliver, Roger Brum, Charlotte Milliner, Simon Lovegrove, Jacob, Stewie & Lillie, Zemo, Sushma Hayes, Mark Foreman, Hollie Horkey & family, Jack Eggers, my friends Bob and Bill, Nancy and Neal, Rocco and Milo.

CROCODILES AT THE WATER COOLER

NAVIGATING THE WATERS OF CHANGE

Jim Peal, Ph.D., John Jodon DBA

Keynotes and Consulting:
www.watercoolercrocodiles.com

All rights reserved. No part of this book may be reproduced or transmitted in any form or by any means, electronic or mechanical, including photocopying, recording or by any information storage and retrieval system, without written permission from the author, except for the inclusion of brief quotations in a review.

Copyright 2018 by Jim Peal, Ph.D., John Jodon, D.B.A.
ISBN: 978-1719320108

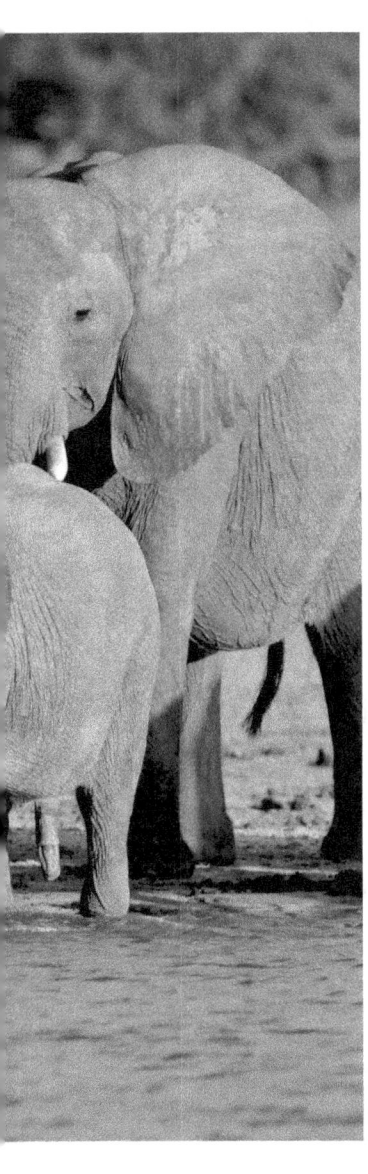

Many people around the cooler may be thirsty but may not have a thirst for change.

Some simply want to quench their thirst then go back to their daily work.

Often unaware of the external competitive landscape, they may not realize that change not a nice to have, change is imperative.

How do you effectively translate this necessity for change into inspiration and engagement that results in actions to enhance your company's competitive advantage?

Leaders want the magic potion that will set them apart from those who fail during times of change — but there is no magic potion, wand, or secret. There never has been.

There is a natural resistance to change in every organization. Some may try to fight the resistance as if they are in a battle at war, some may act like the resistance is not there, but those who tend to be the most successful are the ones who embrace and understand the resistance and work to transform it into a positive energy that moves the cause forward.

The crocodiles around your watercooler are not the enemy, they are your productive employees waiting for your leadership.

What's in This Guide

PART ONE – WISDOM FROM THE PAST **15**
    Three Stories. 17
    30% Factor 23
    The Water Cooler 24
    5 Common Mistakes Leaders Make 25
    Organizations in Change 29
    Communication and Your Impact 32

PART TWO – CROCODILES **35**
    The Nature of Crocodiles 37
    Four Types of Water Cooler Crocodiles 42
        Victimis Fatalis. 43
        Antagonizing Intimidontis 46
        Pompositus Arrogonticus. 49
        Sneering Cynicalicus 53
    The Four Change Allies. 56
        The Eagles 57
        The Beavers. 59
        The Monkeys 61
        The Owls 63
    The Four Crocodiles & Four Change
    Allies Strategies 65

PART THREE – ACTIONS **67**
    Strategies to Enhance Change
    1. Know your culture – Culture Assessment 69
        Purpose/Vision 72
        Identity 74
        Values 77
        Processes 79
        Behaviors 80
        Environment 81
    2. Scope the Change 83
        Transformational and Incremental Changes . 85
        Utilizing the Change Matrix 89
    3. Enhance Communication 92
        Stakeholder Mapping 92
        Building Your Vision for Change 94
        Quality Communication Matrix 97
        Assuming Buy-in 101
        Alignment 104
        The 5 Degrees of Alignment 107
        Become the Crocodile Whisperer 111
        Crocodile Whispering Fundamentals 112
    4. Not Planning for Sustainability 128
    5. Actions to Build in Sustainability 131

WRAP-UP **137**

APPENDIX **139**
    Check Your Tude Chart 139

PART ONE
WISDOM FROM THE PAST

"Some of the best lessons we ever learn are learned from past mistakes. The error of the past is the wisdom and success of the future."

— Dale Turner

Three Stories

Steven

Steven was a CEO of a very successful product design and manufacturing company owned by a parent company. The parent company decided that they wanted to co-locate three of their design and manufacturing companies into one facility and have those three businesses operate as one company. They selected Steven, the CEO of one of the companies, as the CEO of the co-located companies. In preparation for the move Steven developed a comprehensive plan for each of the companies in terms of the logistics for making the move to the new facility. They completed a very detailed plan of where everyone and each department would be located and the layout of the assembly floor. The move went as planned and they initially felt successful. During the whole process Steven assumed that all of the employees were "plug and play," meaning that they all knew their jobs and would resume doing their work once they were in the new office.

The parent company expected that they would realize a greater profit since now these three companies were sharing services and gave Steven a couple of months to effectively multiply the profit margins. Even though each of the three companies had been successful, once co-located their performance actually decreased and the profitability did not meet expectations.

Steven remained optimistic but was oblivious to what was actually happening inside of the office. Even though they were in a brand new modern facility, three distinct groups formed according to their legacy companies. There was a lot of finger pointing and jealousy between the groups. Within a very short time, whenever a problem arose it became a full-out "us versus them." There was tension and dysfunction instead of cooperation and collaboration.

This tension and division was also present in Steven's senior leadership team. The team felt that Steven was not part of the team because he denied the reality of what was going on inside the building. He would often respond to their concerns with, "These things will work out." The members of his leadership team began to have two meetings, one when Steven was present and another meeting after he left the room to deal with the real issues they were having. The discord and dysfunction at the new facility rose to such a level that customers noticed and began stepping in and doing check-ins at an alarming rate. Steven could not figure out why. Products that were normally delivered on time in the past were getting later and later and the customers' concerns and frustration were growing exponentially.

Steven's blind spot extended into his senior team. Most of the team was from the other companies and Steven assumed that they knew their jobs and should be able to continue on as if nothing had changed. He minimized their complaints as "growing pains" they would get over. His dismissal alienated his leadership team members despite his intention for the business to succeed.

It took Steven months to catch on to what was happening and to begin the process to course correct. It then took him and his team about two years to merge the three companies and people into a unified operation. First Steven met with and unified his leadership team. Together they crafted a vision for the company they wanted to be. Then they gathered information from all the different departments in meetings and focus groups to determine what was needed to make them a high-performing part of the organization. Steven held frequent town hall meetings to provide updates and open the floor for questions and answers. He conducted training sessions for his supervisors on how to manage and lead change. His project manager logged all of the integration activities on large posters throughout the building so all of the employees could see the progress in each of the 44 goals they had set for the year.

At the end of the first year all 44 goals had been completed and palpable progress was the result. The good news was that as their integration work proceeded the customers began sending unsolicited letters stating how all of their concerns were dissolved as they witnessed the companies come together. What started out as three companies under one roof transformed into an integrated company where the technologies began to integrate as well, giving the unified company a distinct competitive advantage.

This scenario is a common one where leaders have ideas and make plans for change but greatly underestimated the people dimension of the change. Steven was not unlike many executives who plan changes for their companies. Steven had the best of intentions and did a great job of logistically planning for the move but the people dimension was his blind spot. Once he caught on, his organization turned around.

Karen

Karen, an experienced change agent with strong toolsets, phenomenal people skills and a strong passion for change, had several successful implementations in continuous improvement methodologies in three smaller companies across the country as part of her resume. She recently joined a medium-sized global company. When Karen took on the new role, one of her first projects was to roll out a major change across this global enterprise consisting of 20,000 employees.

Karen assumed that her prior time estimates at the smaller companies were a good benchmark and she could simply multiply the timings by a factor of three for the global change she was planning. Consequently, when she set up her rollout plan, she made a few key underestimations. She assumed that the implementation would be identical at all locations, not taking into account the country-specific differences. She miscalculated the time it would take to get the leaders aligned at all the locations so they could deliver a message that would gain traction for that country. Because she used primarily an organizational chart for each country she missed the nuances that each country culture had and how that culture would impact her efforts. She rolled the change out from the main office and locked all the decks to make sure the same message was delivered at each location.

While she was well intended, the practices were informed by her former company experience. She severely underestimated the time, resources and commitment needed to properly roll out and implement the change. In her previous smaller companies, creating buy-in was relatively easy because all of the critical staff was on the same campus. In her new role the critical staff was spread across the United States, Europe and Asia.

She had a successful big launch event but then the efforts very quickly seemed to fizzle. Timelines started getting pushed back, resources were not at an acceptable level and the workforce quickly started questioning the ability of the process and the leaders driving the change.

After several painful months of not meeting the goals of the change timeline, Karen had to rethink her strategy.

Senior Leaders

The senior leaders of the power company decided they wanted to automate the field workforce by having the linemen enter their work logs on tablet devices. They ambitiously bought all the hardware, installed the top of the line system and trained the linemen on how to use the tablets. The senior leaders thought their job was done.

What followed shocked them. The linemen tossed the tablets into the closets. They grumbled the tablets away as another "great idea from senior management, the ones who don't even know or ask about what we do." They saw no use or benefit in using them and neither did their direct supervisors so the tablets got tossed into the closet. Leaders often falsely assume that their "good ideas" will be automatically put into place as they do not want to take the necessary time to listen to, communicate with and engage their organizations.

This environment of forced change and under-communicated change creates the breeding ground for crocodiles. Formerly productive employees turn into these crocodiles that devour perfectly "good plans" for change and all those plans come to a screeching halt.

The 30% Factor

There are many reasons why only 30% of change efforts reach their intended goals. The lack of quality communication on many levels is the primary reason change fails to stick. The message of change fails to penetrate adequately into the organization. On average, approximately 68% of senior leaders have a solid understanding of what the change entails; that drops to 53% of middle managers and ebbs at a dismal 40% of front-line managers who understand the need for change. With those numbers, imagine how low the percentage would be of the line in the back office and for the shop floor workers.

Leaders often will craft their plans for change without fully engaging the organization in the change process. If a person does not understand what the change is, why the change is happening or have a chance to participate in creating the change, how can that person ever fully make it personal and own the change process?

Leaders architect change for their organization but often forget to take into account the ecosystem where they are introducing that change. They force their ambitious plans on the organization without regard for the people who are there. When this happens the system rejects the change – when people do not accept the change, the change fails.

You will see the 5 common mistakes leaders make when planning and executing change in their organizations and what you can do to avoid those mistakes and increase your chance for success.

The Water Cooler

The water cooler plays a significant role in our offices. You might say it is the connective tissue of the office. It's a place where people have open conversations and speak their minds about the hot topics in the workplace. It's often a place where the truth is told about how people really feel at work about the leadership, issues, projects and deadlines as they seek sympathy or encouragement from their colleagues.

Many leaders don't realize how important conversations around the water cooler are in terms of being a good barometer of what's actually going on in their organization. Leaders often shy away from the water cooler interactions. Rather than manage by walking around (MBWA), they hide out in their offices with "wide open doors" but no one comes in. Nor do leaders realize that the water cooler is equivalent to the watering holes that we find in the savanna, where animals of all types come to nourish themselves.

The quality of the interactions (water) in your business defines your culture. You and the other leaders are responsible for the health of the culture. The people who work for you depend on you to sustain a positive work environment for them to be successful.

Every watering hole has the potential for a crocodile infestation. When the water is clear, most animals can come drink and leave with a degree of safety because they and you can spot danger as it is approaching. When leaders ignore their responsibility to create and sustain a positive culture, the water becomes tainted and ultimately becomes infested with crocodiles.

Five Common Mistakes Leaders Make Regarding Change

People in organizations don't forget. Once a change has failed, it takes much more effort to make it right than to do it right in the first place.

We have illustrated a few examples of mistakes leaders make when wanting to bring change to their organizations. Over the years we have seen that there are 5 types of mistakes that leaders often make regarding change. The good news is that there is something you can do... the cost is the time it may take, and the benefit is a sustainable change. Leaders often want to shortcut the change practices that will increase their odds of having a sustainable change. While urgency is always nipping at our heels, urgency is not impatience or force. You can't ignore the preparation that it takes to make change successful. Better to take the time on the front end rather than suffer the consequences and costs of a poorly planned and executed change. It is the paradox that pays off.

Many of the practices we will suggest engage the organization from the inception of the change and allow for their input and participation to create a change they will engage in and execute.

The 5 Mistakes

1. **Ignoring culture** – Leaders are oblivious, or they ignore or minimize the people in the organization and the importance of having quality interactions. They focus on the tangible aspects of the change like the what and when but forget the importance of the who. Leaders often think that change has to be top down and that the organization needs to be told what to do rather than engage the organization in understanding the need for change and allowing them to actively participate in the formation of the vision, goals and milestones. Leaders may institute change by org. chart rather than getting to know and understand the people in their organizations.

2. **Assuming one size fits all** – Leaders assume that change should be standardized and implemented the same everywhere. They forget that for many changes the "common" elements need to be pared down to the essentials. Leaders are blinded to the specific nuances at sites and locations that may not be able to implement change exactly as it was planned.

3. **Inadequate scoping** – Scope creep is a natural phenomenon when it comes to organizational change. Once you start changing one part of an organization, you may quickly see other parts of the organization that are begging for change or that if left unchanged will block the change that you are planning. Those who have remodeled their home know this phenomenon very well. Leaders often plan too big of a change over too short of a time. Leaders spend so much time designing the change they lose sight of what they are asking the organization to do and create an inadequate expectation

for timelines. While there is always a normal tension for change when the work force is faced with an unreasonable goal and timeline at the start, they may get overwhelmed, discouraged, frustrated or angry and thwart the change effort before it really starts.

4. **Inadequate communication** – Leaders may get a clear idea of where they want to go in their own minds but they "ignore the culture" and do not take the time to crafts a series of vision statements that are fitting for the different parts of the organization. They fall prey to the "one size fits all" philosophy and assume that one message is all that is needed for the entire organization. They also often assume that they are the best ones to communicate the message, rather than understanding who would be the best messenger for different parts of the organization. Leaders often avoid the tough questions that usually are on people's minds when it comes to change. They assume that people are bought in and will execute, rather than ask. Many times we see that leaders under-communicate. They think that once-and-done is enough. They assume the people in the organization will just "get" ideas that they personally have spent months developing.

5. **Not planning for sustainability** – Leaders neglect to consider how the change will perpetuate through time and other changes. They focus on the front end of change but neglect building the change into the systems that will make the change stick.

As you look at the 5 mistakes that leaders commonly make you probably have noticed the interconnection between them. This is one reason why change is a complex topic. It is not simply just checking the box and you're done. Think of your change effort as the living and dynamic organism that you need to get to know intimately and tend to in order to ensure its health and longevity.

Change takes energy. So you need to make sure that you and your leaders are grounded in the principles and practices that will allow them to embody and sustain an energetic attitude and approach throughout the process.

It is no secret that an organization's survival and ability to compete often depend on its ability to adapt and change with the emerging landscape. While this book is focused on change, it is not specifically about how to determine what your market strategy should be. The tools in this book are designed to assist you in preparing for change within your organization without falling into the crocodile's trap. We address these 5 mistakes and provide best practices that will improve your chances of implementing change successfully.

Organizations in Change

People in general want to succeed, but our nervous system is wired to create and maintain habits, so there is an inherent resistance to change that often is not even conscious. For example, you mostly likely tie your shoes in the same way that you learned when you were a little kid. If you want to see how wired in that pattern is, try tying your shoes by looping the laces in the reverse direction. You will see that it is not as easy as it may seem to loop the string in a clockwise or counterclockwise direction depending on what you are used to. So leaders have to consider that a "simple" change may in fact be very difficult to implement because we are wired to make habits.

Often, leaders assume that all they have to do is tell the organization to change, without considering the dynamics of what it takes for an actual person to change, regarding both the task and, often more importantly, what happens internally when we ask or tell people to change. There is a whole inner game to change that leaders need to master if they are to be successful. We are creatures of habit, but there are other factors that inhibit change. When changes occur, a process of unlearning the old and leaning the new needs to take place in each person impacted by the change.

Fear is a big motivating factor in many of the decisions that people make every day. It is not the momentary kind of fear we get when we watch a scary movie or try skydiving for the first time. It is the kind of fear that echoes inside of us and infiltrates our sense of security. People fear becoming obsolete and losing their jobs, ultimately not being able to provide for their family or afford the essentials of living. This is the fear that drives people at times to become irrational or closed-minded, or even to completely turn around and run away!

A VP of Operations decided to change how the product was assembled. Previously one person would assemble the whole unit from start to finish. The person took great pride in being able to take a bunch of parts and make a product that was useful to and valued by the customer and the company. When the vice president decided to create an assembly line, this meant that a person would only be working on one part of the product. It also meant that this employee would have to teach others how to do the other parts of the assembly that they once did entirely by themselves.

The vice president experienced great resistance to this change because the person did not want to pass on their knowledge to others for fear of losing their job. The employee also experienced a diminished sense of pride from the loss of actually making a product from beginning to end. It took quite a while before this employee saw for himself that this change actually made him more valuable to the company.

Even if we know the change being discussed is going to enhance our lives in some way, such as reduce our daily amount of work, give us more opportunity, improve our health or put more money in the bank, the ability for people to overcome the fear of the unknown and accept the change is quite difficult.

Rather than resist resistance, as leaders we need to understand the nature of resistance and the different flavors of resistance and what is underneath driving that resistance. Then we need to embrace people's concerns with open communication. You will make true progress when you address resistance at this rudimentary level.

Communicate, Communicate, Communicate

Gaining a thorough understanding of the reasons why people are resisting the change and then developing a strategy for engaging and addressing their concerns are the first steps to engaging and gaining traction. When the main reason to the resistance to change is a lack of communication, the answer is, obviously, quality communication. Be sure of one thing: you can never communicate too much about change. If you think you have done enough, do more! It will only help your efforts.

Leaders often forget to ask for opinions and perspectives of people in the organization closest to the work and then to truly listen to them as they are planning the changes. While you may encounter all the reasons why the change won't work, their perspectives will be invaluable as you plan how you will actually get from point A to your goals.

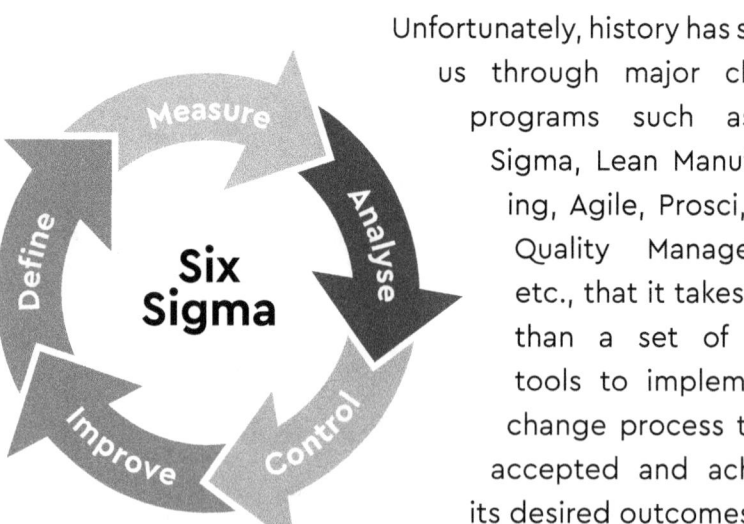

Unfortunately, history has shown us through major change programs such as Six Sigma, Lean Manufacturing, Agile, Prosci, Total Quality Management, etc., that it takes more than a set of good tools to implement a change process that is accepted and achieves its desired outcomes.

While all these major methodologies have made gigantic promises on how a business can be turned around, people and companies still struggle to get any kind of meaningful results or return on investment. The problem is not the actual program. All of the above programs are sound and valuable and have helped many businesses achieve goals. The problem is not the tool, but actually how the leaders handle the people side of implementation.

Whether using one of the above methodologies or just thinking that switching to ½-height cube walls is a straightforward change, most leaders underestimate the people element of the change. Understanding the link between the 70% change initiative failure rate and the prevalence of crocodilian attitudes lurking in the waters of their culture will give you valuable insights on how you can more effectively lead change. The tips in this book help to raise the odds for success of your change, so that your efforts are not the flavor of the day, here one minute and gone the next, but instead create a long-lasting sustainable change that achieves your company's goals.

Our past experience with training thousands of people on change management has taught us that without effective preparation and efficient and ongoing communication and engagement, crocodiles will surface out of the depths of the organization and thwart your attempts to bring about change.

PART TWO
CROCODILES

"If you want to make peace with your enemy, you have to work with your enemy. Then he(she) becomes your partner."

— Nelson Mandela

The Nature of Crocodiles

We can learn about what happens in the office by understanding crocodiles. When the water becomes foul, murky and filled with algae, the lurking crocodile can sneak up on their prey feast and multiply. Before you know it, your watering hole is filled with crocodiles that devour your attempts to create change.

Crocodiles often work in teams to hunt their prey. They are ambush hunters, swimming in a circle around a school of fish and gradually making the circle tighter until the fish are forced into a tight bait ball. Then the crocodiles take turns cutting across the center of the circle, snatching the fish. The larger crocodiles will drive fish from the deeper part of a lake into the shallows, where smaller, more agile alligators block their escape. A larger crocodile repeatedly chases fish toward the shore with powerful splashes of its tail, while smaller, more agile crocs wait in the shallows, ready to snatch the cornered fish. Sound like some office scenarios?

A huge saltwater crocodile might scare a pig into running off a trail and into a lagoon where two smaller crocodiles wait in ambush. In this case, the circumstances suggest that the three crocodiles anticipated each other's positions and actions without being able to see each other.

Crocodiles may look like they are insensitive but the skin of a crocodile is highly sensitive and they are tuned in to the environment around them. They can sense the energy of an organization, team or person, and have an amazing ability to watch and strike at exactly the moment that team or person is most vulnerable. They sneak up on unsuspecting people who are at the water cooler taking a break from their normal work day. If you're not looking out for these types of crocodiles, just like in the wild, they will get you because they're watching for you and they're watching for those moments when you're not paying attention.

When these crocodiles attack your employees, the energy and efficiency inside of your organization automatically go down. People try to act as if nothing happened but everyone is on edge, on alert. When people are on edge their focus is on their own well-being and not so much on the job they need to do. There's also a good chance that those people who are bitten by the crocodiles will turn into crocodiles themselves over time. Negativity is very contagious. It does not take long for an entire organization to become infested with these ominous energies. Not only must you be on the lookout for these energy eaters, but on top of all that you must also make sure you don't turn into a crocodile yourself in the process.

It is not by mistake that the crocodile has been around since the dinosaur age. One of the greatest assets of the crocodile is its ability to be stealthy and patient – able to sit for long periods of time observing the environment and calculating behaviors. These animals are masters at allowing change to happen all around them, while they remain secure, content and thriving on a behavior that has carried them through millions of years. We all know these people. You know...the ones who have decades of service, have outlasted many rounds of leadership and reorganizations. Some may look like they're tough and crusty but actually they're very sensitive and always on the alert. So they will have the upper hand in a given situation unless you come in with the vigilance and intention to engage them and help transform their negativity into productivity.

Don't become a hater

It can be very easy for someone leading change to become infected with Crocodilitis. Remain vigilant and rooted in positive intention. By taking on positive intention, you can create an environment where these crocodiles can return to their true nature of being productive employees.

If you judge these employees as being bad right off the bat, then you are banishing them to negativity forever and you will never give them a chance to come around. It's important that you, as a leader, take on assuming positive intention so you can understand each of these crocodiles and what makes them tick, what the circumstances were that contributed to their becoming a disgruntled crocodile. These people can be your greatest change allies or the most lethal entities that will crush your efforts depending on how you engage them.

Much like the crocodiles at the watering hole, office crocodiles often band together and infect others with their words and actions. By knowing your people, you will recognize the first signs of negativity and can have the conversations that will help productive employees stay productive and help the crocodiles return to their productive selves. Leaders who ignore the signs that communication is needed in the name of "I don't have the time" often pay the consequences later.

What is often unexpected is when well-meaning change agents and leaders who start out enthusiastically with their change plans become the very crocodiles they are trying to avoid. After meeting the inertia and resistance to change that they often encounter, they become set against the members of their own organizations.

Be on the lookout for the signs and symptoms that you may be turning into a crocodile. Emotional intelligence (Daniel Goleman) teaches us how to pay attention to ourselves. Listen to the messages and stories that your inner voice is telling you. Pay attention to your feeling tone – what's in your gut.

It's your job to ensure the environment is a safe place for people to come to replenish and recharge themselves. Your people need to know that you have created a place where they can get what they need to do the work that they're hired to do.

We will explore what makes a normally productive employee turn into a "crocodile" that lurks in the office, snapping at a leader's change efforts, and devouring them before they get a chance to take hold. There are four types of crocodiles that are likely to grow in your organization. Later we'll talk about what you can do to become a "Crocodile Whisperer" who helps transform them back into productive employees.

TYPES OF WATER COOLER CROCODILES

Four Types of Water Cooler Crocodiles

Better to recognize a crocodile and know what to do than to get bitten by one. We will talk about how the four types of crocodiles are born and then later we will share best practices for how you can become the Crocodile Whisperer and transform them back into productive employees eager to engage in the change initiative you have set in place.

Victimis Fatalis

The person who is prone to becoming a Victimis Fatalis starts out as someone who is very collaborative and team oriented. They are very hard working and very warm hearted. They like knowing what to do and having the time and a peaceful uninterrupted environment to work in. They like to be asked their opinion and tend to be very consensus driven when making decisions. They are inspired by being asked politely to help out and demotivated by being tasked dispassionately, threatened or demanded to work. In high-performing teams they will go to great lengths to make sure the job is done. Their warmth engages people and inspires the team spirit. They similar to the Supporters or the Green (DISC) team members. They can turn into a crocodile by forceful and demanding leadership that does not seem to genuinely care. In this type of environment, they feel overpowered and helpless to do anything about it and become the Victimis Fatalis.

Victimis Fatalis, the victim crocodile, looks helpless and deflated. As a result, people are drawn in, thinking they will rescue the victim only to be dragged to the bottom of the watering hole by their infinite energy drain. The victim crocodile drowns unsuspecting people with whining, complaining and excuses.

Victimis Fatalis wants to be successful, but has given up and assumes there is no hope and they are helpless to do anything. This often happens when they are told to change and/or to change immediately. Because the Victimis is not confrontational they will remain in a comfort zone of complaints, gossip and despair rather than risk a major confrontation. They collapse their energy and withdraw. It's a way to stay completely safe despite their complaints.

Because they see themselves as helpless to change things the Victimis think that the negative past will become their future and that they cannot do anything to change their circumstances. They believe they have tried everything, and that is their rationale for giving up. Victimis tend to be resigned, suspicious of people's intentions and envious of what others have. They huddle together and have pity parties at the watercooler, talking in whispers about what is happening in the office. Participating in gossip is one way to know you have been bitten by the Victimis Fatalis. When confronted the Victimis Fatalis will defend their helplessness by giving excuses for not changing.

If you push them too hard you will plunge them deeper into their feelings of powerlessness and they will make you into one of the reasons they can't be successful. A leader can often feel trapped and victimized when bitten by the Victimis. When they bite, you feel your energy draining out of you. It seems like they are draining the life out of your organization as well and you can't do anything about it. Ironically, you then have been victimized by the bite of the Victimis Fatalis.

What makes the Victimis Fatalis tick:

1. They have betrayed their own value and worth but think it is someone else's fault for the way they feel.
2. They project positive qualities outside of themselves and internalize the negative qualities.
3. They think their energy away by not recognizing or acknowledging their own power – this creates an energetic black hole.
4. They feel drained or that they have been robbed of all their energy and you will feel that way too when you establish rapport or talk with them.
5. Giving up is their first thought.
6. They feel that they have no control but in fact they have given up trying.
7. They avoid confrontation – they won't risk saying what they are really thinking but will gossip behind your back.
8. They feel betrayed – wronged or violated – by people's actions and lack of consideration.
9. They have a lot of unspoken rules and a lot of unspoken lines that get crossed.
10. They are like the kid who goes limp when you want to pick them up.
11. Their need for approval, for acknowledgment, for recognition, is never satisfied. They feel that they are fatally flawed.
12. They want someone to come and save the day for them.
13. They often feel like "it's their fault" even when there is no reason.

Antagonizing Intimidontis

The person who is prone to becoming an Antagonizing Intimidontis starts out as someone who is very driven for bottom line results. They are very goal driven and are not concerned about how people feel but rather have a priority on the results that are created. They like to be the person who makes the decisions and calls the shots and being left alone to call the shots. They hate to be micromanaged – being told what to do and monitored closely. They like to state their opinion and tend to be very self-oriented when making decisions. They are inspired by being given full rein/independence to determine the goals and timelines and to drive the organization/team to that goal. They are demotivated by people who don't perform, have excuses and are late in delivering results. In high-performing teams they will drive to getting the job done. Their command helps teams to become focused on the goal and delivery. They are similar to the Directors or the Red (DISC) team members. This crocodile often becomes born when the leadership comes across as weak or indecisive. When the leadership does not take a strong stand for a decision or direction, the loss of respect that ensues becomes the fertile ground for this crocodile. In the presence of weak leaders, they exert their dominance as a way to sustain a sense of control.

The full-fledged Antagonizing Intimidontis are the angry bullies in the organization. They slosh and splash around the watering hole making a lot of noise and showing their teeth. They are angry and frustrated at everything that is not going their way. When they are not making a lot of noise they sit back brooding, waiting until the smallest thing goes wrong, and then they snap and attack any positive efforts that the company and/or leader is making and point out what is not working or any other shortcomings. These adversarial crocodiles always blame others and everything outside of themselves when things go wrong.

They get people agitated and worked up and want everyone to share their hostility and anger. Their noise gets people upset and of course, productivity grinds to a halt. They are experts in playing the blame game, and they try to cloak their hostility and anger with sarcasm. Often frustrated with the situation, they lose all patience and start tearing into others.

The Antagonizing Intimidontis' anger is fueled by a fear that they have lost control and think that they may be at fault. They lay blame to avoid accountability. They get frustrated but are unaware that they have given up on a situation, group or person and now are choosing to make them wrong rather than engage. They would rather be right than do what's right.

If you are conflict adverse the Antagonizing Intimidontis may pose the biggest challenges to you personally. They like to keep people away with their bluster, aggression and blaming.

Because they are so noisy and obvious, they are easy to spot. Later in the book we will give you some tips on how to transform this formidable crocodile.

What makes the Antagonizing Intimidontis tick:

1. They call you out.
2. They point the finger and are very critical, looking for who is at fault. Leaders are the largest target for them.
3. They pressure, attack and intimidate and then make people think they're wrong feeling that way – avoiding their part in creating an unpleasant environment.
4. They focus on what is wrong but don't acknowledge anything positive.
5. They put themselves in a one-up position.
6. They come off as condescending and arrogant, with a puffed-up, inflated self-image.
7. Their one-up position supports their anger about how inferior the world and leadership are around them.
8. They are always looking outside of themselves for fault because they see themselves as faultless.
9. They express their hostility through sarcasm.
10. They will take a defensive posture when criticized or asked to take responsibility.
11. They think they are doing the right thing by raising issues in the way that they do, but often are unaware of how off-putting their mode and style of combative communication is.
12. Their combative confrontations are all in the service to making themselves look capable.

Pompositus Arrogonticus

The person who is prone to becoming a Pompositus Arrogonticus starts out as someone who is very detail driven and wants to do their job right. They are the masters of information and knowledge. They want to make sure that all the data has been collected and that all processes have been followed correctly. They want be the person who is correct and has all the facts; it does not matter how long it take as long as it is done correctly. They don't like rash decisions because they like to carefully calculate their opinion and rely on a complete data set before they will weigh in. They are inspired by having the time to completely research the topic before making a conclusion. They are demotivated by people who spin the facts or just spout random ideas. In high-performing teams they will ensure that accuracy and precision are achieved. Their attention to detail and process helps teams to ensure high quality in their work products. They similar to the Analyzers or the Blue (DISC) team members.

Leadership that subverts or spins facts to get what they want, glossing over them and minimizing their contributions often turns them into crocodiles. It is infuriating to them when a leader does not respect their knowledge and shortcuts decision making by ignoring the facts. When leaders minimize the importance of accuracy or the amount of time and work it takes to have quality and accurate results they will withdraw into a negative state of mind. Leaders who take credit for their work will set this person's trajectory into becoming a crocodile. This person will turn inward and will tend to hoard information and "knowing how to do things" as they change into crocodiles.

The fully developed Pompositus Arrogonticus looks like they're there to help somebody but really this croc just pushes the individual underwater and steps on and over them under the pretense of helping them. They have given up on receiving acknowledgment for what they have brought to the table and have become committed to blowing their own horn.

This croc wants to be wanted and glorified, so after they take over they hijack the credit, claiming that it was a good thing they stepped in to save the day. These crocs may look and sound altruistic, like they really do just want to help, but in reality they are out for self-righteous glory to fill a void they have been feeling.

Even though they see themselves as superior because they "have the facts and know how to do things" they never will let on to others that they think less of them. They hoard information as their power over people. They often think of management as stupid because they don't ask them their opinion.

Managers can easily become Pompositus Arrogonticus when people come to them with their problems. Instead of empowering the person to think through the problem themselves, the manager steps in and either solves the problem themselves or tells the person what to do as a set of instructions. The HBR article "Who's Got the Monkey?" describes this phenomenon clearly.

When you get bitten by the Pompositus Arrogonticus you first have a feeling of elation because you think that help has arrived. Pretty soon you will see the bubbles rising and realize that you are underwater. Their trap is looking like they want to help you but rather than being the true team player, they are out for their own gain and will praise themselves at the end. Pompositus Arrogonticus can also look like the hero; they save the day but intentionally do nothing to support the people to handle it next time.

What makes the Pompositus Arrogonticus tick:
1. They see the world as a place that needs their salvation.
2. They want to appear like they just want to "help," but underneath their seeming kindness is an active subtext that says, "I am helping you because you don't have what it takes, and I do."
3. They minimize the other person's power, effectiveness, skills and talents.
4. They are on the hunt for what is missing, but only if what is missing is what they have to offer.
5. They hold a fundamental judgment of others as being inadequate and incapable.
6. They look like a team player but they are really there to hijack the credit.
7. Unlike the Adversary, who will sit on the sidelines and criticize, they will not hesitate to jump right onto the playing field, take over, and then later, take all the credit.

8. They elevate themselves in the presence of the Victim and validate the Victim's thought that they are helpless and the situation is hopeless but you will save the day.
9. They project themselves as better than all of the other meta-attitudes. But that is their own private secret.
10. They will give you a false sense of hope but really disempower by taking over and leaving you empty-handed.

Sneering Cynicalicus

The person who is prone to becoming a Sneering Cynicalicus starts out as someone who is a very creative big ideas person. Before becoming a crocodile, they love the energy that comes with the big ideas. They can look at a situation and instantly come up with innovations. They thrive in an environment where there is a lot of brainstorming and idea generation with others. They feel that details and processes are buzz killers. Often they will come up with the idea and then move on to the next shiny object, leaving the details of how to get there undone. They are demotivated by people who question their ideas and the thinking that is behind the idea or people who are asking for the process of how to get to the great idea. In high-performing teams they inject a high level of energy and enthusiasm, not to mention ideas. Their creativity helps teams think outside the box and innovate. They are similar to the Promoters or the Yellow (DISC) team members. The leaders who are the dream crushers create these crocodiles. They mock creativity, going around bursting the bubbles of innovation with lines like, "That will never work here," or "That is a stupid idea."

Having their visions and ideas crushed multiple times gives birth to the Sneering Cynicalicus, the cynic who poisons the entire pond with their negativity. They have soured and are negative about everything. They think their negativity is a sign that they are smart. They don't think they are foolish like those visionaries who have high hopes and are destined for demise and disappointment. They think that dashing their own hopes for things to be different insulates and protects them from feeling disappointed by others. They simply expect things not to work out or to change. They are not OK with others who might be happy and will douse any signs of enthusiasm.

At a mining company team session one person said, "My job sucks. The equipment we have sucks. My manager doesn't care and sucks. The mine manager sucks. And I have five years before my retirement and every day is going to suck!" The person next to him raised his hand and said, "I have been here for a year and I think the mine manager has his heart in the right place. My manager is really supportive and I like her. We have an equipment plan and I can see how our tools are getting better. I'm looking forward to my career here." The first guy turned to the second man and with a sneer said, "Don't worry, you'll find out!"

The Cynicalicus just waits for somebody to express some sort of positivity or hope and then extinguishes that hope with a blast of negativity, drowning out any possible chance of something positive. They live to create the motto "Misery loves company."

What makes the Sneering Cynicalicus tick:

1. They are afraid of and avoid disappointment.
2. They don't see their cynicism as intellectual cowardice; they think they are just being smart.
3. They are pretending to be too smart to think anything can change.
4. They think they are too smart to get emotionally involved.
5. They don't believe that anything will ever amount to much.
6. They say no to everything automatically.
7. They hose down any positivity with their poisoned outlook.
8. They are deathly afraid of feeling disappointed so they have decided that it's all wrong and all not worth investing any interest or energy.
9. They have traded hope for passive anger.
10. They are brittle, not tough.
11. They are playing it safe and avoiding risk by never allowing any new energy or possibility into themselves.
12. They are afraid.
13. They pass judgment on anyone who is trying to make a difference and ridicule the efforts of individuals and organizations that are working hard.
14. What comes out of their mouth is poisonous and attempts to shatter other people's dreams so they can join in their lifeless misery of dashed hopes.

The Four Change Allies

Yes, we all need to be on the lookout for the crocodiles that may infest our workplace, but all is not lost. There are many change allies as well. By identifying and then fortifying them you can effectively build a critical mass of positivity toward change.

The following are thumbnails of the four types of change allies that naturally exist in organizations. They are energy points that will help energize the change efforts in different ways. It is best to recognize the strengths that you have in your organization regardless of their title and support them throughout the process.

In the appendix of this book you will find the Check Your Tude table. At a glance you can see the range of positive and negative attitudes found in your change allies and crocodiles. The Four Change Allies and the Four Types of Crocodiles are adaptations of the chart as it can be applied to change initiatives.

The Eagles

The Eagles are the Visionaries in your organization. They have their eyes set on the future and live in the future. They keep us focused on where we are going and why it is important to get there. They naturally inspire people to look beyond the fray of today. When obstacles arise the Eagles remind others of the vision and goals; they know that it is natural for obstacles to occur and that we need to see the goal posts while dealing with the immediate urgencies. Without the Eagles, people's efforts can become scrambled and off course. We need to keep our eyes on the Eagles, who can see the goal from their vantage point.

Work with your Eagles by engaging them in the change vision, both in informing them and seeking their input. Ask your Eagles, "How can I support your success?" If your Eagles stop talking about the future, engage them to find out what is stopping them from communicating about the goals. You can also ask the Eagles to reach out to certain individuals who may not be able to see the big picture.

Eagle key identifiers:

1. They have a visceral feeling about the vision – a deep sense of confidence. For Eagles the vision has a three-dimensional quality to it that makes it very real. Eagles are living and breathing that future vision.
2. They are focused on the destination and direction.
3. They are at the 50,000-foot level and see the big picture, 360 degrees around.
4. They see the interrelatedness of things.
5. They feel the outreaching possibilities of the vision and how this vision interconnects with other people, systems and organizations.
6. They exude appreciation for what is around them.
7. They create an environment everyone wants to inhabit.
8. They don't live in denial, they acknowledge the obstacles that arise and consistently keep everyone focused on where they are going.
9. Because they are congruent in their speech and actions they instill trust in those around them.
10. They bring a sense of inspiration because they build a window into the future that is palpable, filled with passion and excitement for what is to come.

The Beavers

As the Activators of change, the Beavers are busy helping us get from where we are today to the vision of tomorrow. They take action, assign roles and responsibilities, and motivate people to be creative in solving problems and to keep moving forward. Placed between where we are today and the vision of tomorrow, the Activators assign roles and responsibilities and provide that spark to get things done.

Work with your Beavers on developing tangible plans and milestones as well as creating ways to celebrate successes along the way. Ask them to help identify those who seem like they are on the fence or those who are disengaged so that you can work to proactively address those tensions in your organization with them.

Beaver key identifiers:

1. Architecting processes and identifying roles and responsibilities, milestones and action timelines gets the Beavers excited.
2. Beavers bring forth a sense of urgency by having one foot firmly in the reality of today to pull it forward and one foot in the vision of tomorrow providing the pathway, the steps, to strategize and be the communicator to bring people forward.
3. Beavers are very pragmatic and concrete.
4. Beavers are always working toward the goal with relaxed zest.
5. Their positive energy favorably affects the people and working environment. They get things to happen.
6. They are a transformative energizer for individuals, groups and projects.
7. Their mindset answers the question, "How are we going to get there?"

The Monkeys

The Monkeys are the Coaches who are alongside of us to help us do our very best in the day-to-day tasks that we must accomplish. They help us keep the nagging problems off our backs and where we can solve them. Coaches see us as fully capable. They will challenge us in a way that we can rise to the occasion as we step out of our own box of limitations. They don't fall for our excuses but encourage us by truly believing in us. Rather than just giving us the answer, Coaches ask great questions so that we can come up with our own answers and solutions that we can own for ourselves. Coaches allow us to struggle with our challenges so that we grow. Coaches give us quality feedback about what we are doing well and where we can improve. Coaches inspire us with their positive energy.

Work with the Coaches to keep them aligned with the vision and provide them coaching. Create a network of coaching to support the organization to meet its goals and execute the change plan.

Monkey key identifiers:

1. They do not force you into anything. A Monkey (Coach) provides the tools for development, and while this process may have its moments of discomfort, embarrassment and hard work, a Coach does not shy away because a Coach believes that you are able to metabolize your own inner strength and knows that you will naturally grow.
2. Coaches interact with you in a very systematic way to bring forth your strengths and capabilities.
3. Coaches facilitate results by supporting your achievement and development.
4. A Coach is not easy on you and yet despite their demanding nature, coaches are compassionate.
5. A Coach brings forth your best without being harsh or disrespectful.
6. Coaches help you grow and develop and go beyond your fears and doubts.
7. Coaches:
    - help you become capable and confident.
    - see your inner strengths, potential and capabilities.
    - create the environment and stimulation so you can be your best and really shine.
    - see people as talented and capable.
    - speak to a person's magnificence and hold a high standard of performance.
    - motivate people to stretch beyond their normal bounds and do incredible things by believing in them.
    - balance patience with high expectations.

The Owls

The Owls are the Mentors who help us see and extract wisdom from our work so that we can continually become smarter every day. While Coaches help us in our day-to-day work, Mentors work with our long-term professional development. Mentors help us reflect on our situations so that we actually learn from mistakes and pass on best practices to others. Mentors have us step back and take in a larger context so we can see our own patterns and patterns of others. Not only can we gain a deeper insight into things, we can use every experience to gain knowledge.

Support your Owls by helping them integrate with the Eagles, Beavers and Monkeys so they have a clear focus on how they can support a learning organization that will move toward the vision of the future.

Key identifiers of Owls:

1. Owls are deeply committed to the development of the person.
2. Owls sit in a place of looking for patterns of success and patterns that limit.
3. Owls help a person make the choices that will facilitate their growth.
4. Owls are focused on developing a person's knowledge and expertise.
5. Owls do not avoid any situation or pain but rather look for the learning that can come out of it.
6. Owls see their patterns and ask questions that will lead them to discover more about themselves.
7. Owls reveal to people how they are thinking and how they can think differently to evolve themselves.
8. Owls promote others' success, not their own.

The Four Crocodiles
& Four Change Allies Strategies

Identify and actively support the change allies in your organization. Your close attention to them before, during and after the changes are made will help you leverage and support these people who serve as positive energy sources in your organization. Allies are good to bring early in the decision-making process. They will have a perspective on the organization because they are closer to the work and often will have better relationships with more people.

Do not avoid or marginalize the crocodiles; engage them. Talking with them is a good way to understand the tensions, pressures and demands your organization is experiencing. It's always a good practice to ask them what would make the biggest difference for them. This will help inform your planning. It is good to bring in a few crocodiles once key decisions have been made to help pressure-test ideas. If your idea can be shredded by an invited croc, better there and then, than to have your idea demolished after you put it out to the entire organization. If you bring the crocs in too early in the idea generation process, they will shred ideas before they are given a chance.

PART THREE
ACTIONS

"Success seems to be connected with action. Successful people keep moving. They make mistakes, but they don't quit."

— Conrad Hilton

STRATEGIES TO ENHANCE CHANGE

1. Know the culture of your organization

Company Culture

Culture is a starting point that is often minimized or overlooked by change leaders. Sometimes changing the company culture is the goal in and of itself. A poor or unstable culture is toxic to the people in your organization and diminishes moral, performance and retention. Successful change leaders assess the quality of the culture and often intentionally include plans to improve the culture as part of their change management plans.

Many leaders launch into organizational changes without doing a full assessment of their organizations and having a deep understanding of all of the dynamics. You need in-depth knowledge about where the organization is today in relation to the changes that you're proposing for tomorrow. Then you can begin to gauge what it will take for your organization to change.

Culture is the way you think, act, and interact

Company culture is the personality of a company that defines the working environment. Company culture includes the work environment, mission, vision, values and key processes. You can look at how people act and respond to each other as one of the core elements of culture. For example, some companies have a team-based culture with employee participation on all levels, while others have a more traditional and formal management style and culture.

Company culture is important to employees, because workers are more likely to enjoy their time in the workplace when they fit in with the company culture. Employees tend to enjoy work when their needs and values are consistent with those in the workplace. They tend to develop better relationships with coworkers, and are even more productive. For example, if you prefer to work independently, but work for a company that emphasizes teamwork (or has shared office spaces), you are likely to be less happy and less efficient.

> "Culture is what you do when nobody is looking."
>
> Herb Kelleher,
> Chairman
> Southwest Airlines

Company culture is important to employers too, because workers who fit in with the company culture are likely to be not only happier, but also more productive. When an employee fits in with the culture, they are also likely to want to work for that company for longer. Thus, employers can improve productivity and employee retention through a strong culture.

Cultural Assessment

Assess the key elements of your culture, including the following: Vision, Identity, Values, Strategies and Processes, Behaviors and Environment. This assessment will give you a good sense of where you are today and how people will hear your plans for change. The cultural assessment consists of qualitative responses to the questions. If you want a more quantitative output, you could apply a scale to each of the questions (1–5). By assigning a number scale to each question you could electronically deploy the assessment to a larger group to create a cultural scorecard.

Cultural Assessment Dimensions
Purpose/Vision
Identity
Values
Processes
Behaviors
Environment

Cultural Assessment – VISION

A vision isn't necessarily a statement. A vision is a set of ideas that describe a future state. Visions should be aspirational and stretch imagination. They should describe the state of the organization across its functions. A vision statement says what the organization wishes to be like in some years' time. Vision provides guidance about what core to preserve and what future to stimulate progress toward. Vision defines what business we are in, and why. Vision is a destination, and your strategy is the roadmap to get there.

A vision presents a clear idea of the future, is motivating and purpose driven. You can use the following questions to evaluate your vision and likewise to formulate a compelling vision for change.

CRITERIA FOR EVALUATING YOUR EXISTING COMPANY VISION

1. Does it present a clear idea of the future?
   - How well does the company vision statement provide a powerful picture of what your business will look like 3 to 5 years from now?
   - How well does the company vision statement represent a dream that is beyond what most think is possible?
   - How well does the company vision represent the mountaintop of where the company is headed?

2. Is it motivating?
   - Does the company vision create enthusiasm and pose a challenge that inspires and engages people at all levels in the company?
   - Is your company vision statement worded in engaging language that speaks to and engages your workforce?
   - How well does the company vision create a vivid image in people's heads that provokes emotion and excitement?

3. Is it purpose-driven?
   - Does the company vision statement give employees a larger sense of purpose?
   - Is the company vision statement worded in such a way that our employees see themselves as "building a building" rather than "laying stones"?

Actions

Cultural Assessment – IDENTITY

Identity refers to "who" is in your organization. Identity is the name of your team, division, company. It is how you are recognized. Identity can refer to your title. One's identity would also include the type of power that you have in the organization. The type of decision-making rights that you have or don't have would be part of your identity. Identity includes your roles and responsibilities. As we look at the different levels of change, the identity could be a change in somebody's title after promotion, it could be a change of the name of the organization, it could be a change in strategic function, or it could be the new name when two companies merge, in which case typically one company will lose its name and hence lose its identity. Many times when companies are merged, leaders want to retain the name of their legacy company because that's what people identified with in regards to the value of the company.

Let's look at an identity-level shift, for instance when three companies moved into one building. These three companies were all owned by a parent company, but operated as individual companies. When the businesses came into the new building, each one retained its own identity for an extended period of time. While this provided some comfort and continuity for some it also polarized each of those groups against each other. They needed a singular identity to come together and operate as one company.

In long-standing companies and institutions, when a new group forms it often has challenges in establishing itself. Because the organization has become habituated to the "way we have always operated," a new group may find resistance to establishing new methodologies or new decision-making procedures and authorities.

When there's an identity-level shift such as the above example, it's probably the most challenging and most complex when addressing culture in the process. Taking the time to address the overall cultural atmosphere for all involved is the best path to developing a viable plan for laying the foundation to molding the new cultural identity.

QUESTIONS TO ASSESS THE IDENTITY

1. How clear are the titles and roles within the group that you are assessing?
2. How well does the organizational chart represent the company as it is today?
3. How well are people's jobs defined and documented in their job descriptions?
4. How clear is the decision-making structure; i.e., the decision makers and the domain of decisions for which they are accountable? How well is the decision-making structure known throughout the organization?
5. How clearly defined is the bench for the key positions? How are people developed for advancement?
6. To what degree do legacy identifications help or hinder the change you are planning, the overall quality of the interactions between those identified groups?

Cultural Assessment – VALUES

"What we've learned is that the soft stuff and the hard stuff are becoming increasingly intertwined. A company's values – what it stands for, what its people believe in – are crucial to its competitive success. Indeed, values drive the business."

— Robert Haas, Chairman and CEO, Levi Strauss & Company

"Values drive a business" is a theme that is foundational across successful businesses. Core values are designed to capture "how you show up, serve and promote who you are as a business." Great company culture comes from its core values. Values are the core essences that people in the business are inspired to live up to. They often will specify behavioral norms that the people should follow when at work. It is useful to quantify the gaps between the values and the experience of the people in the organization. For example, a company may say that they value people but the people in the organization do not feel valued; they may feel that their value to the company is only monetary.

Actions

QUESTIONS FOR ASSESSING YOUR VALUES

1. How well are the company values known and understood by all employees?
    - How close are people's perceptions about the organization's real values to the stated values?
    - To what degree are people able to link the company values to specific behaviors?
    - How visible are the company values in the common area?
    - How frequently do you hear people discuss the values as they relate to their work?

2. Values are incorporated into decision making.
    - To what degree are the company values a definitive guide for everything you do?
    - To what degree are the values a decision filter for hiring, developing people, customer decisions, growth and strategic decisions, etc.?
    - What percentage of behavior and decisions are consistent or inconsistent with the values?
    - How well are your values seen as core to the business? Seen as one of the critical success factors?

3. To what degree are the values reflected in the stories employees tell about work?

4. How well/frequently are the values recognized, rewarded and celebrated? Used as a basis for hiring and firing?
    - Recognition of an employee is an opportunity to showcase the values and connect what they did to a specific company value.

Cultural Assessment – PROCESSES

This category refers to how we do the work to achieve our goals. This can be one of the most common types of business change we can make. There are numerous process assessment models and tools, especially if you are in the manufacturing space. The questions below are not meant as a replacement for a more formal process assessment that you might conduct.

In general, the following are a few broad-brush areas to assess your culture in terms of processes:

1. **Effective** – How well do your processes enable you to meet customer requirements?
2. **Known** – To what degree are your critical path processes known by the members across your organization?
3. **Established** – To what degree are the processes mapped/documented?
4. **Efficiency** – To what degree do your processes maximize resources and time while preserving quality standards?
5. **Engagement** – How well are the people aligned and engaged, and how well do they follow the established processes?
6. **Change** – How well does your organization recognize when a process needs to be improved? Is it able to methodically make improvements to its processes?

Cultural assessment – BEHAVIORS

Behaviors are what we do. Behaviors are very easy to recognize because they are objectively observable. Some examples: Smiling and saying hello to people I see in the hallway, sending an agenda before every meeting, distributing minutes.

TO ASSESS THE BEHAVIORS OF THE ORGANIZATION

1. How well do the behaviors of people demonstrate the values of the company?
2. How well are the defined work processes actually followed?

When we think about leadership behavior during times of change, it's essential to realize the effects that your non-verbal behaviors and words can have on an organization. Organizational ears become more in tune and organizational eyes become crisper when watching the behavior of those leading the change process. Remember that as leaders and change agents, we are always being watched for how we will handle situations, barriers, setbacks and successes. During times of emotional upheaval that change often brings, leaders and change agents cast a shadow that can either influence positivity or increase the opportunity for the creation of more crocodiles in the business. When you talk negatively about the change process, the people or the reason behind the initiative, you potentially create a situation of negativity that will flood the organization. Keep a focus and express word of positivity, whether dealing with a small setback or a major readjustment of the change plan. Just as important will be the type of behavior and language you use during times of success. It cannot be stressed enough how important rewarding and recognizing the team and organization can be for all wins during times of change. This is the time to set the example, to lead by example and cast the shadow of authentic positive leadership.

Cultural Assessment – ENVIRONMENT

The environment represents the physicality of where people work and also includes the relationships that each person has.

1. How well does the physical environment reflect the vision and values of the company?
2. How conducive is the environment to getting work done?
3. What is the level of:
    Cleanliness?
    Visual order?
    Open space?
    Natural light?
4. What is the emotional tone of the organization?
5. What is the quality of the relationships?
    1. Level of trust
    2. Quality of communication
    3. Ability to resolve conflicts

4. Working as a team
5. Collaboration
6. Quality of corrective feedback
7. Quality and frequency of praise and validation
8. Appropriate level of management (micro – hands-off)

2. Scope the Change

LEVEL OF CHANGE \ CHANGE MATRIX	SCOPE OF CHANGE				
	INDIVIDUAL	TEAM	GROUP	DIVISION / BUSINESS UNIT	COMPANY
PURPOSE/VISION					
IDENTITY					
VALUES					
PROCESSES					
BEHAVIORS					
ENVIRONMENT					

Transformational — T Incremental = I

Scoping the change helps to remedy both mistakes about assuming one size fits all and obviously inadequate scoping. Scoping the change automatically has you examining how the change will land in different parts of the business as well as different geographic locations. After you have completed your cultural assessment, you can use those dimensions to further clarify the change that you are proposing by filling out the Change Matrix. Utilizing the Change Matrix, a preparation tool, will guide you in many dimensions of the change:

1. The Change Matrix will give you a deeper understanding of the nuances of each area expected to change, which will inform how your proposed change will need to be modified to fit in the various areas of your company. This allows you to:
2. Make the change relevant to the various business areas and geographies (not assume one size fits all).
3. Better size the change.
4. Inform your communication plan.
5. Serve as a focus point for leadership and organizational alignment.

Transformational and Incremental Changes

On the vertical axis of the chart identify the highest level of change that you are proposing, and then on the horizontal axis of the chart select the breadth of the change that you are proposing. In that box you will place a "T" or an "I."

T – Transformational change means a change that is moving to something that is completely different from what exists today – a large magnitude of change.

I – Incremental change is a change that is delivering more of the same. If I'm adding one more metric to an established set of metrics, that would be an incremental change. If I'm proposing a completely different type of metric system that's going to replace the old system, that is a transformational change. Adding to existing metrics would most likely be considered an incremental change; implementing metrics where they did not exist before would be considered a transformational change. The power company always had consequences that included termination for people who violated safety policies. When they started actually terminating people who violated the policies it was a transformational change for the organization.

You want to be able to distinguish between transformational changes, which are much more complicated than the incremental changes, which usually are easier to accomplish. Having this distinction will help you better estimate the amount of time it will take to fully execute the change.

Your completed Change Matrix will also help you in both content and style when you're preparing the communication messages to the organization. So often leaders present the same message to the entire organization when a tailored message for specific groups would have created a much bigger impact. The detail that will come out of this exercise will allow you to step more fully into the shoes from different parts of your organization.

When it comes to standardizing your change you will be making decisions as to how wide and/or how deep the standards will be implemented. On one end of the spectrum, if you have to apply the same change everywhere, the change matrix will inform you of the challenges you might face in certain part of the organization. These nuances are invaluable as they will allow you to properly estimate the amount of time that will be needed and the implementation timelines for your plan.

The IT department of a global pharmaceutical company was planning to roll out a global desktop. While there were hundreds of applications that were used in the organization that were supported by IT, they decided to standardize the desktop with eight applications that were universal. This structure allowed for consistency and created the space for each function to add the applications locally that would support their business.

EXAMPLES OF TRANSFORMATION AND INCREMENTAL CHANGES

Attribute	Incremental	Transformational
Source	The past and present i.e. what we know	The future, and a commitment to bring that into reality
Focus	Content	Context
Process	Linear, present to future	Discontinuous, Future to present
Style	Predominantly about management, i.e. Change Management	Predominantly about leadership and being 'unreasonable' inside the current circumstances
Our experience	We know it well	Requires new learning
Speed	Slow	Rapid
Results	Predicable	Unpredictable and breakthrough

1. If one person is being promoted in title only and will have the same reporting structure, this would be an identity-level change and an individual scope. This would be an Incremental change for that person. If a person is being promoted to a VP level and now will manage several functions instead of one team, this would be a Transformational change for that person. It would not necessarily be a transformational change for the organizations under that leader unless the new leader is going to change those organizations.

CHANGE MATRIX

LEVEL OF CHANGE	SCOPE OF CHANGE				
	INDIVIDUAL	TEAM	GROUP	DIVISION / BUSINESS UNIT	COMPANY
PURPOSE/VISION					
IDENTITY					
VALUES					
PROCESSES				T	
BEHAVIORS					
ENVIRONMENT					

Transformational — T   Incremental = I

2. If a leader is planning on doing a reorganization of all of his/her divisions, this would be a Transformational change for all of the organizations impacted.

3. If a leader changes the vision of a company, it could be an Incremental or Transformational change, depending on how different the vision is.

Example of filling out the Change Matrix

Let's say you are planning to change a major process for an entire division. You would put a T in the box that corresponds to division and process change. From that box down and to the left will indicate the boxes where you would gather detailed information about your change. In the box where the T is, fully describe the end state or goal for the change that you are intending to create. As you are crafting this end state think about the key groups you will be presenting it to. This information will come out of your Key Stakeholder Map (described later). If you draw a horizontal line across and a vertical line through the acts and fill in all the boxes to the left and below those two lines, you will find all the boxes that need detail.

Filling in each of the boxes below that line and to the left of that line will give you a greater amount of detail and understanding of what you'll be asking your organization to do. If it's a division that you're making the change for, then you need to have an understanding of how each of the groups and/or teams in that division will be impacted by the change you're proposing. As you are looking at each box, determine the level of granularity that is best for the change you are making. If there are several hundred teams, then you may want to group them by function or by geography or by both to bring out the information that will be most relevant for understanding and communicating about the change.

Filling out this level of detail is best done by your leadership team and their direct reports because they can give a more accurate view of what that change means to their organizations. They can take the matrix further into the organization to get more granular input. A best practice is to ask your leaders and managers to take this matrix all the way down to the line organization and allow people on the line to have an understanding of what the changes are and ask what those changes would look like at their level. By giving people lower in the organization the opportunity to contribute to the description of the change, you'll have a greater level of buy-in from those people in the organization.

While this process does take time, it is a time investment that is worthwhile. Slowing down for this process will allow you to go faster later. By taking the time up front to complete this matrix you will accomplish many of the foundational elements for success. Not only will you be more fully informed, but the organization will have a reference point that will inform and guide the change.

Some of the questions you can fill in for each box in the matrix can include the ones listed below. The idea is to create questions that will give you the necessary information needed to implement the change in each division, team, geographic location, etc., specified in the overarching change.

Some of the questions can include:

1. What is the starting point?
2. What does the goal look like?
3. What is the evidence that will let you know the change is completed?
4. What are the key milestones?
5. What needs to be taken into account for the implementation of this change?
6. What are the key challenges that must be addressed?
7. How should the challenges be met?
8. How long will it take to make this change?

9. What are the key messages that need to be communicated – to whom, how and when?
10. Who are the key people accountable?

Counting the number of blocks covered in your change will give you an idea of how much energy it will take to make the changes. As a rule, Transformational changes take more energy than Incremental changes.

Filling out and completing this matrix is not a small task. It becomes a living document that serves as a baseline and changes as the design of your change matures. Once the timelines are gathered you can have a project manager apply the milestones and timing to a spreadsheet so that you and the leadership team can look at what it will take for your change to take place. Having this broad view will also let you adjust your timelines to allow for all of the emerging priorities that always occur.

The completed Change Matrix informs your communication strategy and specific messaging and gives you a sense of how much energy it will take to have success. Your leadership team will gain many insights from the data that is collected and put into the Change Matrix.

3. Inadequate communication

Mapping the Key Stakeholders

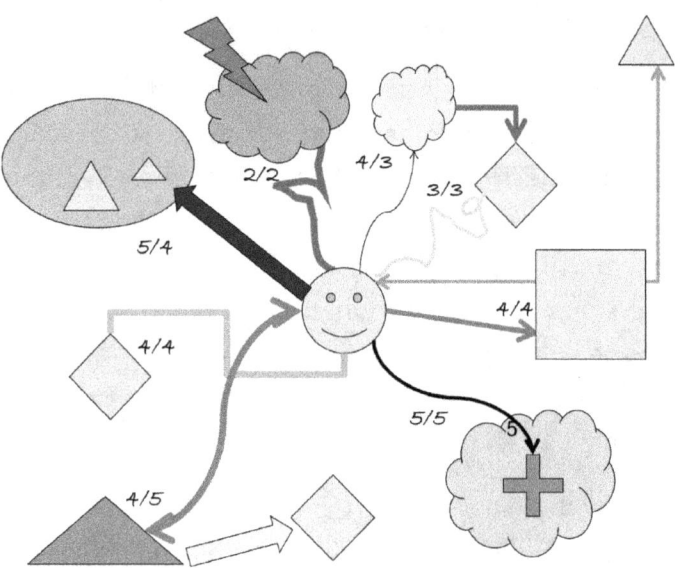

When considering the people involved in the change process, a useful tool to help you gain a new perspective on your organization is a map of your key stakeholders regarding the change.

First, write a list of the key stakeholders for the change that you're about to implement. The Change Matrix can inform this list. Then take a large piece of blank paper and create a map of your key stakeholders. Place yourself in the center and then visually represent the key stakeholders around you—individuals or teams/groups or a person inside of a team or business unit; spatially locate them to represent the proximity to you, either work-wise or physically. Then add connector lines between you and those entities and between the entities as well. The connector lines can represent the quality of the relationship by its thickness, color, smoothness/jaggedness, etc. Then assign two numbers to each key stakeholder to indicate the level of alignment: the top number is from your point of view, and the second number is from their point of view and their experience of you.

When you're done, you'll have a visual map that will give you a new perspective on all of your key relationships. This map will inform the creation of your vision statement and your communication strategy. Notice what all of the higher-rated relationships have in common; same for the lower-rated ones. As you look at each relationship, think about what you can do to sustain the healthy relationships and what is needed to transform the ones that need improvement as you create your relationship strategy and plan. You may also sequence your relationship plan in terms of which relationships need the most attention at what points in the change process. In other words, you may have a relationship that has a low rating, and that is OK for the next 9 months; for example, after which that relationship will need to be enhanced.

Creating your stakeholder map is another process that can be done with your team to create an aligned view and strategy for approaching and engaging the organization.

Building Your Vision for Change

Your vision for change becomes sharper having completed the Change Matrix and the Key Stakeholder Map. The Change Matrix grounds the ideas you have in the reality of where your organization actually is and its capacity to change. Your vision statement is a written document that includes a clear description of the end state and goals and the benefit it brings to the company, its customers and its employees.

Building an aligned change vision is challenging because it requires the alignment of your leadership levels for the two levels below you and needs to link to the overall strategic imperatives of the company.

Your change vision should be a coherent and powerful statement of the desired future state. The leaders at the top two levels impacted by the change should have the same vision and definition of the future state. It is then the responsibility of those leaders to identify their key stakeholders, map them and modify the message so that it lands for those groups as relevant and meaningful. Their responsibility is to create a compelling change story that all their employees can relate to. The story is adapted to fit each unique level and function that it applies to. This initial investment to get your leaders aligned will pay off in the future rollout of your change initiative.

When you are writing the change vision statement you will be writing several statements: an overarching statement and numerous statements that are tailored to the key stakeholders (informed by your map). You also want to consider the crocodiles in your organization in terms of the messaging that will help engage them in the change.

Vision statement elements to include:

1. What the change will look like when it is complete. What's different about the company, what's different about the business units, what's different about how that part of the organization or the entire organization operates or functions.
2. What exactly has changed.
3. What the evidence is that shows you have been successful in making the change.
4. What people will see, hear and feel after the change is complete. What is different for the different areas of the business and locations.
5. What is changed in terms of how people get their work done.
6. What is possible as a result of the change that wasn't possible before.
7. What's in it for the organization overall and then more specifically what's in it for each individual person.
8. What the deliverables of this change are – such as a plan or operating manual or a set of procedures.
9. When this change will be complete.
10. List of the key accomplishments along the way; the milestones.

Assess the vision statement thoroughly and collectively, and review the project based on the clarified vision and crafted strategy:

- The objectives and key elements of the project/program/initiative;
- Clarity around what it means for the program/transformation to be successful; can lead to discussions on some specific implications for groups and people;
- Clear statements on the desired performance and improvements that will result from the change/transformation;
- Prioritization and integration of the program with other ongoing (and potentially competing and/or duplicating) company programs/initiatives;
- Builds on your company's history, strengths, unique capabilities and assets.

Getting the vision clear is the first step. Without clarity in your vision, everything else that follows is more difficult. As you are crafting the versions for your key stakeholders, step into their shoes and ask, "What is important and meaningful for me?" Using this frame will allow you to create the linkage they can relate to and align with the vision.

As you develop your vision it should generate a strong, positive, compelling feeling for your leaders. They actually have to FEEL this vision in a powerful way. If your vision produces a bland response in your leaders, it needs more work to make it compelling. The people in your organization are going to be responding to the energy of those who are communicating the vision. If you are not passionate and clear about the change, they will follow your lead. This energy needs to be sustained throughout the change process, not just at the beginning. Your leaders will need to call on this energetic core as they face and resolve the challenges that are sure to lie ahead.

Clearing the Waters with Quality Communication

Clear, regular communication sets a definite direction; quality communication keeps the water clear. Leaders leading change forget to communicate. They think that being clear is enough. They have put so much time and energy into their plans they forget that the majority of the organization has not been along for the ride. Often leaders become impatient with the communication process. They may feel frustrated with resistance and resent it instead of expecting, embracing and transforming it. They forget that they have to "use their words" to create the future for the organization and will have to repeat the same messages hundreds of times to get through to the muscles of the organization. Leaders rely on their fancy PowerPoints to do the trick instead of just talking to their people.

INTENTION VERSUS IMPACT

Pay attention to how people are reacting to you. Rather than defining communication as your intent and the message sent, define communication as the message and impact that is received. You need to understand that your message and impact is what the other person hears and feels regardless of your intention. In other words, your communication is the response that people have to what you say and do. If people are confused, demotivated or angry at what you have said, you need to look at how your message created that impact first. It is too easy to blame the receiver when, in reality, the message you sent is the cause. Making this fundamental switch in your perspective expands your ability to be an effective communicator by giving you more choices in how you communicate.

After a meeting or two or a couple of all-hands meetings to announce the change, leaders often think that they have done their job. Not so. Announcing a change is not communicating and nowhere near creating the alignment necessary to implement change successfully.

Use the following guide in terms of an ongoing strategy for managing quality communication:

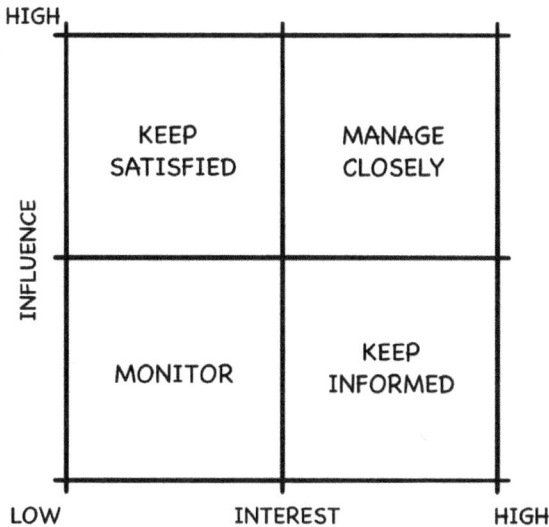

Once your map and vision for change is complete you can group the people and groups in the categories in the diagram in order to determine the best strategy for communication. Those with high interest and high influence; i.e., the ability to influence what gets done or not done, would call for a customized communication that is tailored specifically for that stakeholder. Conversely, someone who has low influence and interest might best be managed with more generic general updates that would be sent to a wider group.

A strategic communication plan helps avert the normal resistance to change. Once you launch your change, don't retire to the office patting yourself on the back expecting the change to roll out as planned. Be prepared for the resistance to the change so that you can minimize your frustration with the people who seem to be dragging their feet. Resist the temptation to reflexively become forceful and even intimidating about the change effort. You can be direct and instill a sense of urgency without becoming a crocodile that menaces people and teams.

We stated earlier that communication can be defined as "the response that you elicit"; that is, you know that you have communicated when your message and its impact is repeated and passed on by the members. It takes work to adequately communicate and create alignment. There are no substitutes. Everyone is looking at the leadership during times of change for their guidance and support as well as for holding the organization accountable for making the change.

When senior leaders waver from owning the change, that attitude will ultimately roll down through the different levels of the organization. There is really no quicker way to end the pursuit of a change process within an organization than to have the senior leadership disengaged in the process.

People need communication in times of change; not just a little communication, but a lot of communication – much more than you might think would be necessary. They need to know the destination, the key points of interest along the way, and feel commitment and support all the way through. They need to hear it over and over again. They need to hear the good and the bad. There is always a little bit of bad in every large change initiative. It is just part of the package. For the most part, though, the bad is temporary. Most of the bad is related to the pains of going through a new stage of learning and adapting to a new norm while still ingrained in normal business activities. You can reframe the "bad" parts in terms of the greater benefit you are moving toward. You can speak it without being of it. Verbalize the hurdles and pain points from a place of neutrality and position it inside of being part of the process. This will let the members know you are aware of what they are going through and not issuing commands for change from the tower. Sarah would say, "Making this change will feel like we are moving backward at times. It will feel like a waste of time. But that is a small price to pay now in terms of gain we will get when the changes are complete."

Leaders should plan on weekly 20- to 30-minute check-ins with their direct reports. Ask them what they are working on and how you can support them as key questions for the check-in.

To get to that place of neutrality and positivity, transform your own negative attitudes into positive ones before communicating to your organization. The Check Your Attitude table in the appendix is a powerful tool that leaders can use to transform their negative attitudes into positive ones. Once in a positive mindset, they can address the resistors and transform their resistance.

Assuming Buy-In

While standing in line to check in to my hotel in Nigeria, I struck up a conversation with the man behind me, who as it turned out was going to be attending the leadership course that I was leading the next day. He asked me about the content of the course. I mentioned that aligning your team was one of the topics. He said, "I know my team is aligned." I asked him how he knew they were aligned. He said, "Because they are all vice presidents." I asked him, "But how do you know they are aligned? Have you asked them?" He stopped in his tracks and just looked at me. Several weeks later I saw him again at another event. He came up to me and said, "You were right. I needed to ask them because as it turned out they were not aligned."

As you think about crafting your change initiative there's nothing more important than creating buy-in. But what really is buy-in? Buy-in is when people can take ownership of an idea. They become the source of the idea. So when we talk about buy-in as related to change initiatives we have to really be thinking about getting people on board and owning the change – to get people to believe in something that is game changing.

Leaders often are baffled when their change initiative stagnates for no apparent reason. Many assume that organizational changes are on autopilot and will continue on their own. They often don't ask themselves, "Have I adequately and consistently communicated to create alignment for this change?" Our response to this assumption is to provide a robust set of communication and awareness tools that better enable leaders to navigate the murky waters of resistance to change.

Change can be either designed and rolled out from the top of the organization or created using an organizational and team-based approach. When change comes from the top, much of the time the senior leaders assume that their ideas and plans for change will be automatically bought into by the rest of the organization.

Sometimes leaders demand buy-in rather than taking the time to create an environment in which participants have the opportunity to express their thoughts and feelings about the proposed changes.

Using a team-based method to designing the change will yield a higher degree of buy-in because people are engaged in creating the change. While it may take more time on the front end, using a team-based approach often results in a smoother rollout.

While success early in change processes is normal, these successes can be the result of direct attention by leadership to certain parts of the change process. Issues occur when problems arise that divert attention from that urgency. A test of the level of buy-in is how people respond after the urgency is dealt with: do they pick up the change activities or are they derailed and distracted from the change initiative? Developing a communication strategy and plan is essential for success.

As mentioned before, at any point when you think you are effectively communicating a message regarding change, ramp up that communication by a multiple of five! It is easy to think that change is being communicated effectively and efficiently and that everyone is on the same page. Communication can always be improved during times of significant change; enough is never enough.

Alignment

Getting buy-in is a little like being a salesperson. Those promoting the change have to be able to sell all the good points of the change process and how it will improve people, places and things.

Often leaders will gloss over creating alignment and engagement for the change and resort to simply telling people what to do or what will be done. They often shrink away from opening a conversation that may surface resistance to their proposed change.

In the HBR article "How to Deal with Resistance to Change," the authors cite a study where they had a "no participation" group that was simply told what to do differently. The "total participation" group was engaged to talk about the need for cost savings and then asked how that could be accomplished. Once they were aligned, training took place. The results were what you would expect: The output of the no-participation group dropped immediately to about two-thirds of its previous output rate and stayed low. Crocodiles were created immediately. They reported immediate resistance and marked aggression against management. They had a 17% quit rate. The total-participation group had a small dip in productivity but quickly rebounded and exceeded previous productivity rates. There were no signs of hostility toward management and retention was sustained.

So what is the difference between agreement and alignment? So often in meetings people try to get agreement when what they really need is alignment. Alignment means that everyone is clear on the outcomes. Agreement is when your opinion matches somebody else's opinion. In order to create alignment, you need an environment where people can disagree with each other and express their views, ensuring that everyone's view is understood and heard but not necessarily agreed with. In order to have a critical mass for moving a change through the organization, each leader needs to work on the two layers below them. This takes work, time and skill.

A vice president in charge of a pharmaceutical factory in Puerto Rico was trying to get his engineers to participate in a two-day alignment meeting. They were grumbling about wanting to take so much time. So he had them take this drawing and calculate the resultant force.

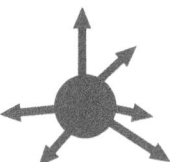

They came up with this:

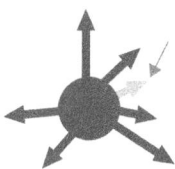

Then he said, "I want you to line up all the vectors and calculate the result of that vector."

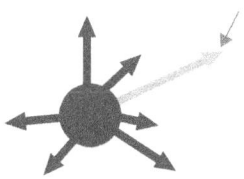

When they did the calculation, they realized there was a sixty-four-fold increase in the length of the vector.

He then said, "That is why I want to have a meeting, so we can get aligned, so that our energy will take us further." His engineers, convinced by the calculation, agreed it would be a good idea to have the alignment meeting.

You should focus on creating alignment with your direct reports and their direct reports—two layers below you. Your direct reports will take it one layer deeper, and so on and so on, to the people down the line. Using the strategy of working the two layers below, the leader gives that leader the amount of direct contact that will be meaningful and create traction.

Alignment is created through conversation. To be successful you must be able to master having alignment conversations.

A tool that can help you assess the degree of alignment is the 5 Levels of Alignment.

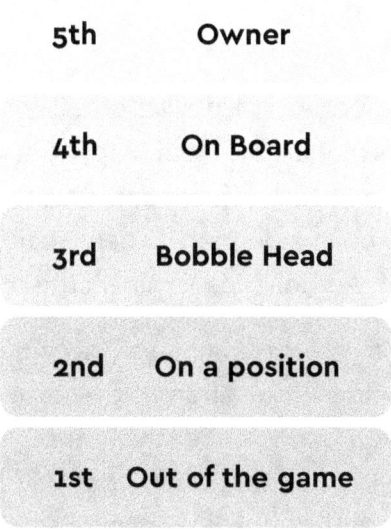

5 Degrees of Alignment

Ideally we want to initially get a critical mass of people to Level 4 or Level 5. The first step is to assess where you are, and then you can assess those around you.

Level 5 is the 'I'm all in!" place. Your energy and enthusiasm is full. You feel that you own the change and in effect are a source of the change.

Level 4 is the "I got it and will go with it" place. It may not have been your idea but you see how it will work and are behind it.

Level 3 comes from the power company. The Bobble Head has not decided whether they are in or out BUT wants to look like a team player so they bobble their head like everyone else is doing or what they think the leader wants.

Level 2 is when people have something specific on their mind that is in opposition to what is being proposed. They may verbalize their concerns or may remain silent. Either way they are against what is being discussed.

Level 1 is when people are dialed out. The lights are on but no one is home. They are not tracking what is going on at all. This can be for a multitude of reasons, personal issues at home, thinking about their workload. Their resistance is passive because their non-verbal cues diminish the focus of the others.

You need to be aware of where you are regarding the issue. Your level determines your energy level and if your energy is not at a 4 or 5, you cannot effectively lead. Part of emotional intelligence is self-awareness. Get what you need to get yourself to a 4 or 5, whether it is conversations, getting your questions answered, voicing your opinion. Once you are at a 4 or 5, then you can lead an alignment conversation. You will need to create the mental safety for people to be where they are and the willingness to engage them in conversation.

5 Conversation Strategies

Level 1 – In private, as soon after you notice that they are checked out, say, "I noticed that you were not your usual self in the meeting. Usually you participate and engage in the conversation. I was wondering if there is something I can do to support you." This lets them know in a non-confrontational way that you noticed them and that you value their contribution and that you care about them

Level 2 – Repeat their objection out loud. You can even write it on a flip chart or board where they can see it; then ask, "Am I understanding you correctly? What else? Does it seem like I am understanding now?" Then you can decide if you want to handle the topic right then and there or take it offline. The purpose here is to let them know that their message has been heard, understood and respected. Writing it is another way to validate what they have said.

Level 3 – Say, "OK, thumbs up if you are yes, thumbs down if you are no, thumbs in the middle if you are not sure right now." The point here is to give space for them to go to Level 4 or Level 5 or to a Level 2. It's better to have them disagree than to not know where they stand. If they go to a 2 then you can use the Level 2 strategy.

Level 4 – Say "How can I support you? What do you need?"

Level 5 — Say "How can I support you? What do you need?" and you might ask, "I noticed that Bill is struggling with this issue. I'm wondering if you could talk with him and see if you can address some of his concerns or surface what is really on his mind." In this way you can have the system take care of itself rather than think that you need to make all of the communications.

It is through self-awareness of where you are at with a particular topic, getting to a Level 4 or Level 5, when you can engage your team and then create the safety and the time to really talk with people. This process will bring about true alignment that is not a forced compliance or intimidation.

Become the Crocodile Whisperer

TAKE CARE OF YOURSELF

So often we are so distracted by our work and pushing for results that our blinders are on for what is going on around us. This is how many leaders become crocodiles themselves in their day-to-day interactions. Often leaders get bitten because they are not aware of themselves or they get caught off guard and get bitten.

Pay attention to how you think and feel. When you are leading change you need to take special care of yourself, mentally, emotionally and physically. Rest and eat well, focus on having a balance with your home life – do some fun stuff. If you find yourself getting short-tempered at work over the change initiative, take a breather, talk to your colleagues to get the support you need to carry on. Listen to your employees and keep asking for their input.

Earlier we looked at the four types of crocodiles and their characteristics. Now we will share tips on how you can transform them back into productive employees eager to follow through on the change initiative you have set in place.

Actions

Crocodile Whispering Fundamentals

What can you do as a leader to prevent crocodiles forming in your organization? A strong, healthy organization doesn't breed crocodiles. Leverage the four types of key strengths: Visionary, Activator, Coach, Mentor. Make sure that they're robust and balanced inside of your organization.

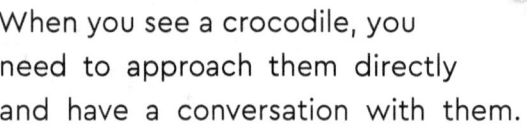

When you see a crocodile, you need to approach them directly and have a conversation with them. Conversation is the primary way that you will transform a crocodile into a productive employee. Often it is not just one conversation that is needed. You must see a crocodile as a productive employee for whom something has gone wrong in their work life, and it's your job to understand that and provide the opportunity for them to tell their story and help them get back on track to being productive.

You can assume that inside of your organization nobody really wants to be negative. What they need is leadership who will listen to them and provide a way forward for them to get back to their positivity. Seeing this as your primary role will help you approach and engage the crocodiles in your organization, whether they are the victims, the adversaries, the rescuers or the cynics.

Stop labeling crocodiles as negative people and see that there is a positivity that they're just not able to fully implement and express inside your organization. You've got to see this is the fault of leadership and not the employee in order to really, truly assume positive intention. Of course, it will be up to them to change their minds, and if they choose to continue to be negative once given the opportunity to shift, then other measures need to be put into place. But again, most of the time crocodiles are created inside of organizations because there's a disconnect that is not attended to.

It takes courage, patience and skill to have real conversations with a crocodile. One of the faulty assumptions leaders have is they don't have the time to talk with people. A company with undiscussed issues and concerns is a breeding ground for crocodiles. When you don't take the time on the front end to talk with your people, you will spend hours later in conversation trying to get to the same place that a 10-minute conversation would have taken you on the front end.

Often it is only after the fact that leaders realize that not having the conversation on the front end when the symptoms were there will take much more time on the back end. You may end up needing to have that conversation with five people instead of one person because that first crocodile bit and infected other people in the organization.

Once you're able to identify what type of negativity or resistance a crocodile is experiencing, then you can hone in on the underlying cause. So often another person's negativity seems overwhelming because we're not able to identify what is truly causing the problem. The resistance may be coming from something in the person's past that has raised uneasy feelings. The negativity could also be a result of the way the change is being rolled out or from crocodiles within the business. Regardless of where the negativity stems, always make sure that you address your own attitude first and foremost. Assume a positive intention and you will be more likely to create a positive impact.

Keep in mind that some people aren't aware that they're creating a negative impact or resistance to change because in their own mind they think and feel that they're just doing their very best or have positive intentions. And they are positively intended; it's just that the way that they're communicating isn't creating a positive impact. This is a fundamental idea that you want to hold that'll keep you assuming positive intention about that particular individual.

Once you've identified the type of negativity that person is into now that you're in a neutral or positive mindset, then you can begin to approach having a conversation. So having a conversation starter or conversational on-ramp is a good way to approach the person. Think about what your opening will be. Typically, you want to start by saying something authentically positive about the individual. Then ask about their work. How are you doing? How is work going? What is your experience on this project? What do you think about the change?

There are a multitude of open-ended questions that you can ask that will give space to that individual and also give you the space to become aware of where they are coming from. Let them know that you understand where they are by repeating back to them the essence of what they have said. Not paraphrasing in a mechanical way but more from a place of curiosity and interest. By listening to the people in your organization you will gain credibility and traction. Show a true sense of caring and compassion.

You can use the Check Your Tude chart in the appendix to identify all of the different mindsets that might be going through your organization in a given time. If somebody's coming across in a negative way and is having a negative impact, you can begin to identify whether they're in the victim row, the adversary row, the rescuer row or the cynic row. Identifying what type of crocodile you're dealing with, what type of negativity, will help you employ the best strategy to help that person shift and change their mind. Most leaders will shy away from conflict because they don't know how to identify what type of conflict it is, and they don't have a clear set of tools that will enable them to confidently engage in a real conversation with the person.

You likely have heard the story about the thousands of starfish washed upon the beach. A little boy is walking on the beach and he picks up a starfish and throws it into the ocean. He takes a couple of steps, picks up another starfish, and throws that one into the ocean. A man approaches the boy and says, "You realize you're really not gonna make any difference, there are too many." The boy takes another step, picks up a starfish, throws it into the ocean and says, "I made a difference to that starfish." Having this attitude that you're going to transform your organization from crocodiles into productive employees one conversation at a time is the mindset that you want to take on.

Strategies for Transforming Water Cooler Crocodiles

Actions

Victimis Fatalis

Victimis Fatalis wants to be successful, but has given up and assumes there is no hope and they are helpless to do anything.

TIPS FOR DEALING WITH VICTIMIS FATALIS

Unwittingly they will try to draw you into their world of helplessness. They look helpless and deflated but their impact can be powerful. They may have the proverbial "Kick Me" sign on their back and it may be easy to feel either drained or frustrated and angry at their attitude. To inoculate yourself against their bite, first, see them as powerful and capable. They do have a powerful effect and although they may have a powerless veneer, that is how they are channeling their power.

The Victimis, in their hopelessness, has lost sight of the positive future, so you want help guide them to get in touch with a positive element of the future.

1. Have them write the goals and vision they want even if it seems impossible to them at the time.
2. Have them do a review of their strengths and accomplishments in writing.
3. When they say, "I can't...," say, "What would happen if you did?"
4. Work with them to take action. Once they can see a

glimmer of positivity in the future, then it is about taking small steps toward that future. The Victimis must take steps, even if they are small, toward a positive future to get out of a victim attitude.

5. Have them write a list of small steps they can take toward their future.
6. Let them know you are there to support their success but it is up to them to take the steps. You can help them brainstorm steps the can take.
7. Don't do anything for them; let them take the actions even if they ask you to do something for them.
8. Help them recognize their steps forward, even if they want to dismiss progress; insist on acknowledgment to what is working.

Antagonizing Intimidontis

Tips for dealing with the Antagonizing Intimidontis

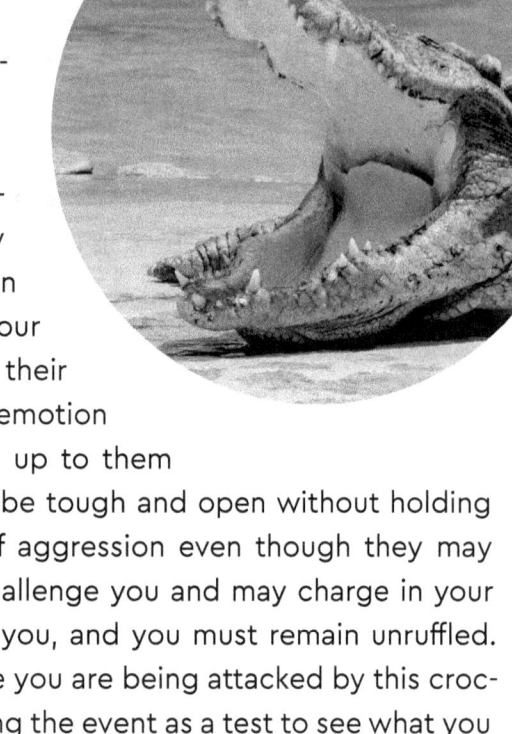

The Antagonizing Intimidontis has a high energy level. Underneath their bluster they want to accomplish things and they fear personal failure. When engaging them keep your energy high to match their level but don't match the emotion of anger. You must stand up to them and not waver. You must be tough and open without holding an intention or energy of aggression even though they may provoke you. They will challenge you and may charge in your direction and/or snap at you, and you must remain unruffled. You might think or feel like you are being attacked by this crocodile instead of interpreting the event as a test to see what you are made of. They respect courage and strength. Resist making them wrong for their bluster. If you get angry and attack them, you have lost the battle. They want results and you want results so help them focus on the results they want.

1. Ask them, "What are you trying to accomplish?" This question awakens the Activator.
2. Ask, "What needs to happen now to make progress?"
3. Ask, "How can you support _____ to move things forward?" What coaching can you provide for them? What would be the best way to approach them? This question helps them to reframe their role as coaches to those who seem to be blocking the progress.

These questions will help the person shift to a productive state of mind. It helps to assist them to step into the other person's shoes. From there they can possibly coach the other person. The adversary will try to take you off course with these questions so you must remain steadfast in redirecting and re-asking the questions until they answer them.

TIPS FOR COACHING ANTAGONIZING INTIMIDONTIS:

1. Help them see how their reaction to this situation or person is blocking forward movement.
2. Ask, "How do you think that _____ feels when you approach them in that way?"
3. Suggest that they argue the other person's point of view first rather than just opposing them.
4. Ask them to verbalize the positive intention of the other.
5. Have them notice if they use sarcasm rather than offering a constructive comment.
6. Challenge them to acknowledge people twice as much as they criticize them.

Pompositus Arrogonticus

TIPS FOR DEALING WITH THE POMPOSITUS ARROGONTICUS****

The Pompositus Arrogonticus is hungry for praise, so authentically acknowledging them is a good way to open the conversation and will catch their attention. Let them know that you value their expertise and that you want to see them pass on their knowledge to others so that they can take on other important work that only they can do. Then shift to asking them to come up with a plan to pass on their knowledge to others. Let them know that you will follow up with them in a week to review their plan. As you shift the frame, show passing on knowledge to others is what you are looking for in terms of moving people forward and up in the organization. Another option is to build into their performance plan; knowledge transfer with specific metrics. Reward progress when you see it by acknowledging them.

Sneering Cynicalicus

The Sneering Cynicalicus may be a tough person to deal with because they are so armored with negativity. They are a disappointed idealist. They have the experience of being disappointed with people and systems multiple times, so many times that they have literally given up hope and are angry at the world for letting them down and angry at themselves for being disappointed. While the Victim has given up and feels no energy, the Sneering Cynicalicus has a cold anger and bitterness about the world. They are saying, "See, I told you it would not work out."

When approaching them, speak to their ideals. You can say something like, "It's clear that you have a definite idea of the way things should be. Tell me about that." And, "It's also clear that people need to be thinking and working differently than they are today. From your point of view what is missing?" Then enlist them in mentoring the people in a positive way. Ask, "What is a way that we can motivate people to grow and do things differently? Would you help me make these communications, keeping in mind we need to motivate people not criticize them?" This will help the person make the transition to the Owl/Mentor. As they get engaged in helping others think and work differently, they will start to feel better. Their final transition is to get in touch with their vision for the organization and to begin communicating that vision to others.

The transformation of the Sneering Cynicalicus is not a short one. They will need lots of enforcement especially when people make mistakes. Helping them take on the Mentor role and reminding them that they need to motivate people to get better or to think differently will help counteract the tendency simply to put others down in a critical and judgmental way.

Remaining vigilant

All animals need to come to the watering hole at some point in time to get water. And when they are approaching the watering hole, and when they're drinking the water, that's when they're going to be the most vulnerable—and that's when crocodiles will attack. It's your job to ensure the watering hole is a safe place for people to come to and that your organization or department is a place where they can get what they need to do the work that they're hired to do. To do this, you need to be on the lookout for crocodiles at your watering hole.

As mentioned earlier, crocodiles may look like they're tough and crusty but actually they're very sensitive and always on the alert. So they will have the upper hand in a given situation unless you come in with the vigilance and intention to transform their negativity into something positive. If you judge these crocodiles as being bad right off the bat, then you are banishing them to negativity forever in your mind and you will never give them a chance. It's important that you, as a leader, take on assuming positive intention so you can understand each of these crocodiles and what makes them tick.

Each of these crocodiles came into the organization as a productive employee and something happened to them over time to turn them into crocodiles. By taking on this positive intention, you can create an environment where these crocodiles can return to their true nature of being productive employees.

Communication Gap Paranoia

Everyone knows the feeling you get when the business leaders or your boss sends out an email scheduling a department meeting. It does not take much to get the rumor mill rolling. When you get the inkling that change is coming and the requisite amount of quality information is not given, you get that feeling way down deep in your stomach that basically tells your brain, "This is not going to be good!" Then the "ripple in the pond" effect follows. It goes a little something like this... "Chris, did you hear that there are going to be some changes going on around here?" Or, "Brenda, I heard that the leaders are talking about implementing a change management program in the company." Or, "Steve, I just heard that we are merging with company ABC. So, what do you think that means about us?" "You know what happens when they do that! People start losing their jobs!"

Slowly but surely, mass hysteria starts to swirl and undermines morale and productivity before anyone truly knows any facts about the change. In the absence of quality information, people make up stories to fill the void, and human nature is to make up horror stories to scare everyone. Everyone hits the panic button and goes into fight-or-flight mode. They will fight you, be frightened of you or just freeze up.

Being proactive means that you provide quality information and keep people engaged from beginning to end. You need to strike a note that resonates with the people in your organization in a meaningful way and that note will be different for different people. This is where the company must ensure that there is a clear and accurate vision of what change is coming and that the leaders are adept and prepared to translate that vision to the different constituents in their organizations.

We asked leaders if they felt they were good communicators; the majority said yes. But how much of your communication is formulated from your listeners' point of view and focused around what is important to them? Most of the time we communicate about what is important to us rather than to the person/people we are talking to. You, or your leaders, need to know your people, and the people need to know their leaders. Because we are in a rush to make changes or improve our businesses immediately, we often gloss over the human connection that will fuel a successful change.

Becoming a great communicator takes time and, most of all, a willingness to put out as much information as needed to keep the business informed on the proposed changes. Willingness is a primary characteristic that leaders often lack when it comes to communication. Most leaders are busy trying to run the business and complain that they don't have time to set up town halls or other major meetings to pass down the critical information of upcoming organizational changes. The leaders either feel that the information they have already passed down is sufficient, or they assume the leaders below them will take care of that more medial work. There are several bad things about that mentality, but probably one of the worst is that during times of change, the employees look up to their leaders for guidance, reassurance and an overall direction of what is to be heading down the pike.

Sustainability

Every leader of change wants to see their changes outlive the ravages of time and the daily fires that will distract attention and effort away from their intended changes. They also want their changes to outlast the crocodiles that will certainly emerge. However, crocodiles have been around for a long time and they are not going away. The challenge in sustaining any type of change occurs when we successfully implement a change and think that things are OK to drop our guard, only to have old habits and patterns creep back in.

One thing that has become increasingly evident is that change can be a slow process that happens at the top first, drops to each individual level below and finally begins to work back up from the workers themselves. The only way sustainability will occur is to make the change important to as many individuals as possible. Working a top-down approach is nothing new to change, but at times the opportunity for distraction from other areas of the business can pull a leader's attention away from the change process. The best way to guarantee a change will withstand the test of time is to have it owned through all levels of the organization. If the senior, mid- or lower-level management lose ownership in the process, the entire infrastructure can collapse, which could cause almost certain loss in any sustainment work.

As we have talked about, those who have turned into crocodiles within an organization are the ones that typically have the hardest time dealing with change. How can you use the strengths of the crocodile to help your company sustain change? If done properly, there is the opportunity to convert even the most seasoned change disrupter into a highly supportive ally. What is your strategy to win those people over? This will only be accomplished by identifying opponents of change and targeting their keen senses and working to address their fears and concerns. Addressing any concerns immediately and on a continuing basis may be one of the best tools you have to help people adopt and sustain the new change process. That is part of what it means to be a Crocodile Whisperer.

Your employees are looking up to you and the other leaders for you to set the stake in the ground and for guidance especially around managing the changing priorities that will most certainly arise. You will need to remind the employees that change is not something new or a one-time event, but rather an ongoing process to be continually embraced. While you have the big picture of change, remember that this vision needs to be translated into a personal journey for each person impacted by the change. What does each person need to be successful throughout the change and into the future?

How can you make change a personal victory for each person in your organization? Remember the WIIFM – what's in it for me. Give employees the guidance and communication they are looking for in regards to what is happening, as well as an understanding of why it is happening and the benefit to them – in their language. That message is best delivered by someone who works closely with that person or group. The better job you do as change agents at offering this context to the members of the business, the better chance of eliminating crocodilian behavior that might prevent the change from being sustainable.

Next are best practices that will help you solidify the changes you made and build a culture of empowerment and ownership.

Five actions to make your change sustainable

1. Verbally reward and acknowledge those who are sustaining the change including promoting the benefits of the change to the customer, the company and the employees.
2. Address issues as they arise.
3. Incorporate change updates into meeting agendas.
4. Document changes into the standard operating procedures.
5. Add the actions that sustain the changes into the annual goals.

VERBALLY REWARD AND ACKNOWLEDGE THOSE WHO ARE SUSTAINING THE CHANGE

Everyone at work likes praise and acknowledgment. It only takes seconds to inspire a person, team or workgroup with your kind words. In times of change and when people have been pulled from their comfort zone, make sure they know they have done a good job and that you appreciate them. Don't assume they know they are appreciated… show them. When you praise them, they glow and will pass that on to their work mates and their loved ones at home. Reward, high five, pat on the back, fist bump…it's all good! Don't be afraid to praise good deeds in public forums. Praise employees in meetings, bulletins, company newsletters, etc.

Steps to make your verbal acknowledgment powerful:

1. Be specific – tell them exactly what they did and the impact they had. Example: "I really appreciated how you ran the kick-off meeting. You followed the agenda that you sent out. You inspired all of us by speaking to the

value each of us brings to the team and created clarity around our roles and timelines."

2. Let them know the impact on you personally. Example: "It made me feel valued and included and motivated to do my best."

3. Let them know the impact of their contribution to the team, organization or company. Example: "Not only did your kick-off motivate me, but I see how everyone is energized and how our accomplishments will serve the entire company."

Verbal rewarding can become a strong asset to building team confidence. There are other types of rewards, though, that can be equally strong at assisting in the sustaining phase of change. While it is not necessary to always offer monetary rewards, they do have a strong place in successful organizations. Monetary rewards can take several shapes. There are the cash rewards, of course, but rewards can also take the shape of a vacation trip, company apparel and paid time off. The main key here is that company leaders need to implement some type of reward system. During my career, I have heard about reward systems in all my companies, but rarely saw anything implemented. This is a discouraging and morale-killing situation, especially for a team or company that has broken the fears of change to build a better company.

Promote the benefits of the change to the customer, the company and the employees

Spread the good news! Perceptions from the outside can be very valuable in reinforcing your change efforts. Receiving unsolicited letters from customers stating that they noticed positive changes in the company and expressing increased confidence in the organization should be shared with all. This type of communication is a great way to continue to build momentum and gain additional buy-in. Read those letters to the leadership team and in all-hands meetings to validate the efforts the organization was making in changing. Repeatedly acknowledge the team for rising to the occasion to make the changes over the longer term that the customers noticed.

ADDRESS ISSUES AS THEY ARISE – BE THE CROCODILE WHISPERER

While we may want to make fun of crocodiles or act as if they are the enemy, ignoring them makes things worse. Organizational crocodiles often become the spokespeople for the issues that normally arise in the face of change. Employees frequently base their votes on whether to accept the change by watching how the business leaders handle the crocodiles. This is why it is so important to win over the crocodiles rather than wage war on them. So, by understanding the ways of the crocodiles that are around the watering hole, we can approach change in a different manner and get the buy-in needed to ensure sustainable success. Many people have transformed into crocodiles as a result of being through many failed changes in the past and/or being given promises that were never kept or acknowledged. People learn from experience. Promises are always being made during times of significant change and if those promises do not come true, the crocodiles will defend themselves from their disappointments and pull others under along with them.

So to be most successful with trying to set up organizational change sustainability, we must address those crocodiles' feelings and concerns as they emerge and not ignore them when they come up for air. The key is to pay attention and engage them in the ongoing change. A person who is part of the change begins to feel ownership and value in what is happening. You can see that as you engage in the change them rather than just telling them to change, they can become willing to change and help sustain the new outcomes.

INCORPORATE CHANGE UPDATES INTO YOUR MEETING AGENDAS

Keeping up with regular updates to the organization is paramount. Keep the change agenda front and center in the minds of your leaders. Your direct reports can in turn repeat the same practice down into the organization. When you and your team carefully attend to the verbal and non-verbal signals that emerge when you are talking about the change initiative, you can pick up on issues that they may be reticent to bring up.

Watch for the eye-roll, the deep breath, the looks that two or more people give each other in silence – just call it out as you see it and bring that conversation into the room. You can say, "I just noticed that you shook your head, what is up for you?" Or, "I noticed that you both just looked at each other, what is that conversation about?" By inviting their unspoken comments into the conversations and acknowledging the issues where they fell out of alignment, you can proactively work to keep your leadership team crocodile free.

DOCUMENT THE CHANGES INTO STANDARD WORK

One way to sustain any size change is to develop standard operating procedures. These procedures allow the business to document the changes that were involved in the development of the new process. These standard operating procedures (SOP) become the foundation for how the business should conduct day-to-day operations. This step should begin and finish during the final stages of the change process and incorporate as many people in the business as possible.

Taichii Ohno says, "If there is no standard work, there is no real improvement." There is a lot of power in this saying and it is also one of the key reasons for the 70% failure rate of improvements that we have continued to address throughout this book. Standard work is about developing a best-case process that allows everyone involved to get on the same page.

Here are some of the key benefits that come out of the creation of standard work:

- Standard work is the process of detailing all steps completely and in a manner that allows all employees to understand the process.
- Standard work allows everyone the opportunity to perform a process or procedure the same way every time.
- An outcome of instituting standard work is an increase in value-added work and a decrease in waste.
- The end process or product becomes predictable and easily meets customer satisfaction.
- There is a reduction of stress on the workers due to standardized training.
- When everyone is performing a process the same way, problems are easier to identify.
- Standard work allows the easy audit of processes to ensure optimization.

ADD THE ACTIONS THAT SUSTAIN THE CHANGES INTO THE ANNUAL GOALS

This may sound obvious and/or easy but you may encounter resistance to adding a new type of metric to the established set of metrics used for measuring performance and rewards. Adding the change and sustainment effort into employee and leadership annual goals and objectives can put a level of ownership and accountability into the process. We have seen that type of organizational resistance emerge. Sometimes leaders will have "leadership/contribution to change initiatives" as a subcategory reserved for formal recognition of change participation. If you experience resistance on this level, look for short-term options that you can reward your team with. Often there are discretionary funds/checks that can be issued to reward your team.

WRAP-UP

Leading change is not a straightforward process. It is messy and complicated and impossible to do alone.

You have seen the role the water cooler plays in our offices, and what you can do to make sure this connective tissue is healthy and will support the growth you intend. We have touched on some tips and best practices that you can use immediately to improve the likelihood of success. Know your people and your organization. Talk to your people; they need your hands-on personal leadership. They need to know that you know what they are experiencing and that you truly care about them. Engage those who seem disenfranchised and help them get back into the fray. Don't hope for a silver bullet because it is your personal support and leadership that will motivate your teams to success.

APPENDIX

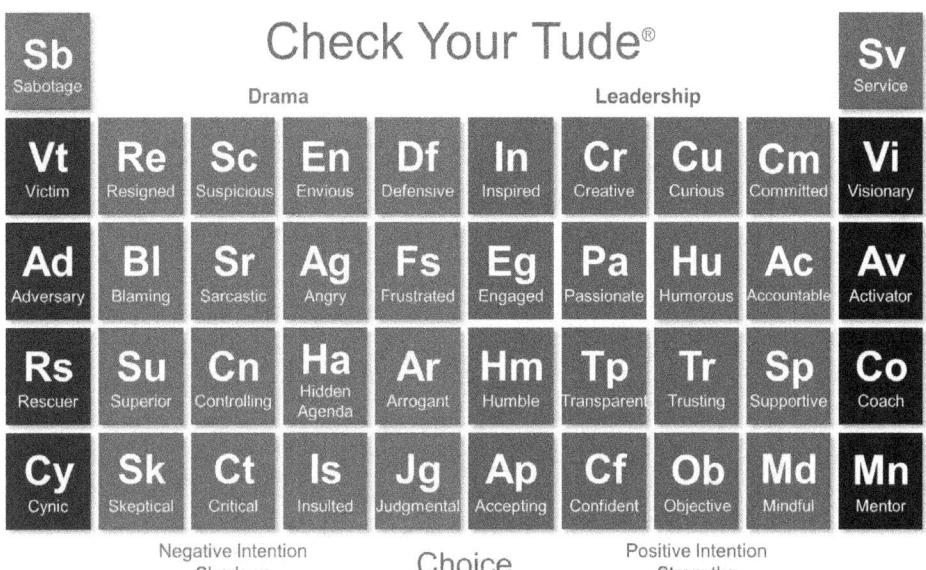

Go to **www.checkyourtude.com** for more detailed information on the chart.

Jim Peal and John Jodon are available for keynotes, workshops and change management engagements.

Go to:

www.watercoolercrocodiles.com

for information.